Investing Workbook Series: Stocks ① ② ③

How to Get Started in Stocks

Published by John Wiley & Sons, Inc., Hoboken, New Jersey.
Published simultaneously in Canada.

For general information about our other products and services, please contact our Customer
Care Department within the United States at 800-762-2974, outside the United States at
317-572-3993 or fax 317-572-4002.

Wiley also publishes its books in a variety of electronic formats. Some content that appears in
print may not be available in electronic books. For more information about Wiley products,
visit our Web site at www.wiley.com.

ISBN: 0-471-71957-9

Printed in the United States of America
10 9 8 7 6 5 4 3 2 1

Introduction

There is no doubt that investing in stocks is a worthwhile endeavor. Over the long term, no other investment type has performed better.

Unfortunately, investing in stocks is not easy. Numerous things need to be learned before you can understand what buying a stock really means. Anyone can pull up quotes and blindly trade, but it takes much more effort to become a true investor. We aim to make this effort as painless as possible.

The goal of this workbook series is to set you on the path to becoming an informed, educated stock investor. We can't promise you will make millions in the stock market next year after purchasing and going through these workbooks, but we can say with certainty you will gain knowledge that will provide you with a solid base from which to start your stock-investing career. You and your family's finances should be better off as a result.

Though the three books in this series are designed to be used with one another, they can be used individually and are of increasing difficulty.

Workbook #1, *How to Get Started in Stocks*, is intended for readers who are totally new to investing. It will help those with little to no stock-investing experience quickly get up to speed on the main concepts. The book explains why you should consider investing in stocks in the first place, what a stock actually is, and the basics of how a company works, and it also answers many of the other common questions new investors might have.

Workbook #2, *How to Select Winning Stocks*, is much more focused. It details how to read a company's financial statements, how to locate quality companies for potential investment, and how to actually go about placing a value on a business. New investors should certainly go through Workbook #1 first, while those who have bought stocks before will probably be fine skipping straight to this book.

Workbook #3, *How to Refine Your Stock Strategy*, is the most advanced of the series. Even experienced investors proficient in analyzing companies may find this an enlightening read into how we think about stocks at Morningstar. In this book, we touch on the investment styles of some of the great investors of our time, share some of the insights and strategies we here at Morningstar have come up with, and finally offer pointers on building and maintaining a stock portfolio.

Each workbook lesson is divided into four distinct sections as outlined below. As you will see, going through these workbooks is intended to be an interactive experience.

Lessons: The main text of each lesson is designed to give you an overview of a particular topic, along with plenty of real-life examples and tips for putting your newly gained knowledge into action while investing.

Investor's Checklist: These scannable lists provide you with the most important take-home messages from the lessons. Use the Investor's Checklists to brush up on what you've just learned and as a quick reference of the most salient points to remember.

Quizzes: The quizzes help ensure that you've indeed mastered the key concepts in the lesson. Answers to each of the quiz questions are at the back of each book.

Worksheets: The worksheets are designed to help you put the key concepts of each lesson into practice. A worksheet answer key is also at the back of each book. Though there is sometimes no right or wrong answer to these exercises, the answer key will in these cases reinforce the points being made.

In addition, each workbook has the following at the back:

Additional Morningstar Resources: Morningstar's Investing Series is designed as an introduction to Morningstar's approach. We have numerous other products for stock investors of all experience levels.

Recommended Readings: This is a list of some of Morningstar's favorite books about stock investing.

Investing Terms: Though each lesson assumes no previous experience in investing (beyond reading the previous lessons in the series), the Investing Terms section gives more in-depth definitions of the main terms used in the text.

While this investing series will be of most value to those who have the most to learn, even the most seasoned investors will find parts of it enlightening. After all, one can never learn too much when engaged in an intellectual exercise.

Good luck on your journey, and may happy returns follow your effort!

Acknowledgments

Developing this workbook series was a collaborative effort with scores of Morningstar people deserving credit. There may be only one name on the back cover, yet all the following stock analysts deserve special thanks for contributing significant portions of the content contained within:

Ryan Batchelor
Joel Bloomer
Eric Chenoweth
Sumit Desai
Lauren DeSanto
Mark Hugh Sam
Toan Tran
Jerome Van Der Ghinst
James Walden

Product manager Alla Spivak shepherded all the books in this series from start to finish, making sure we hit our deadlines. With three books in the pipeline at once, her juggling was impressive.

Superstar copy editor Jason Stipp worked very hard to make sure the prose was clear and the grammar correct. Many of his weekends were spent making this a better product. Morningstar's design staff, notably Lisa Lindsay, Christopher Cantore, Victor Savolainen, David Silva, and David Williams, developed the books' design melding ideas and words into a pleasing format.

Former director of securities analysis Amy Arnott and chief of securities analysis Haywood Kelly provided time from their busy schedules to give valuable feedback in the editing process. They made sure all the bases were being hit and that the messages were consistent with the Morningstar framework. David Pugh, our editor at John Wiley & Sons, also provided valuable guidance.

Morningstar's director of stock analysis, Pat Dorsey, deserves thanks for creating and molding the investment philosophy and concepts we have distilled here. I also owe a large debt to Pat as well as all of the stock analysts on Morningstar's natural resources team for affording me time away from my "day job" to create this series.

Catherine Odelbo has earned a tip of the cap for developing the series' concept. As leading architect and head of Morningstar's Individual Investor business unit, she has always carried the torch for Morningstar's "Investors First" motto. Of course, I'm incredibly grateful to Morningstar founder Joe Mansueto. This is all possible due to Catherine and Joe's vision, leadership, and true belief in the value of independent equity research.

Finally, the books in this series could not have been written without sacrifice and understanding from my family. To them, I owe a special debt.

—*Paul Larson*

Contents

Why You Should Invest in Stocks

Lesson 101: Stocks Versus Other Investments   3

Lesson 102: The Magic of Compounding   13

Lesson 103: Investing for the Long Run   23

Lesson 104: What Matters and What Doesn't   35

Digging into a Company

Lesson 105: The Purpose of a Company   45

Lesson 106: Gathering Relevant Information   55

Lesson 107: Introduction to Financial Statements   67

Lesson 108: Learn the Lingo—Basic Ratios   81

Nuts and Bolts of Stock Investing

Lesson 109: Stocks and Taxes   95

Lesson 110: Using Financial Services Wisely   107

Lesson 111: Understanding the News   119

Lesson 112: Start Thinking Like an Analyst   131

Lesson 113: Using Morningstar's Ratings for Stocks   145

Additional Morningstar Resources   157

Recommended Readings   159

Industry Web Links   162

Quiz Answer Key   165

Worksheet Answer Key   175

Investing Terms   185

Formulas Reference   215

Why You Should Invest in Stocks

Lesson 101: Stocks Versus Other Investments

"Some regard private enterprise as if it were a predatory tiger to be shot. Others look upon it as a cow that they can milk. Only a handful see it for what it really is—the strong horse that pulls the whole cart."—Winston Churchill

We all have financial goals in life: to pay for college for our children, to be able to retire by a reasonable age, to buy the things we want. Unfortunately, spending less than we earn is typically not enough for us to reach our goals. We have to do more; we have to invest our savings and put our money to work. Stocks are quite simply one of the best ways to make your investment dollars work the hardest.

Investing in stocks is not rocket science. The only real characteristics shared among successful stock investors are basic math skills, a critical eye, patience, and discipline. Combine these with an understanding of how money flows and how businesses compete with one another, along with a dash of accounting knowledge, and you have all the mental tools needed to get started. We will teach you all these in this workbook series.

Although you don't need an advanced college degree to invest in stocks, selecting stocks is nevertheless an intellectual exercise. It requires effort, but it can bear many fruits. After all, investing in stocks not only leads to potentially higher returns on your investment dollars, it also leads to a greater understanding of how the world works.

What Is a Stock?

Perhaps the most common misperception among new investors is that stocks are simply pieces of paper to be traded. This is simply not the case. In stock investing, trading is a means, not an end.

A stock is an ownership interest in a company. A business is started by a person or small group of people who put their money in. How much of the business each founder owns is a function of how much money each invested. At this point, the company is considered "private." Once a business reaches a certain size, the company may decide to "go public" and sell a chunk of itself to the investing public. This is how stocks are created.

When you buy a stock, you become a business owner. Period. Over the long term, the value of that ownership stake will rise and fall according to the success of the underlying business. The better the business does, the more your ownership stake will be worth.

Picking Stocks   If stocks are ownership interests in businesses, selecting which stocks to own is really an exercise in picking which businesses you want to own.

Why Invest in Stocks?

Stocks are but one of many possible ways to invest your hard-earned money. Why choose stocks instead of other options, such as bonds, rare coins, or antique sports cars? Quite simply, the reason that savvy investors invest in stocks is that they provide the highest potential returns. And over the long term, no other type of investment tends to perform better. (Lesson 103 will talk all about the historical returns of stocks.)

On the downside, stocks tend to be the most volatile investments. This means that the value of stocks can drop in the short term. Sometimes stock prices may fall for a protracted period. For instance, those who put all their savings in stocks in early 2000 are probably still underwater today. Bad luck or bad timing can easily sink your returns, but you can minimize this by taking a long-term investing approach.

There's also no guarantee you will actually realize any sort of positive return. If you have the misfortune of consistently picking stocks that decline in value, you can lose money, even over the long term!

Of course, we think that by educating yourself and using the knowledge in this workbook series, you can make the risk acceptable relative to your expected reward. We will help you pick the right businesses to own and help you spot the ones to avoid. Again, this effort is well worth it, because over the long haul, your money can work harder for you in equities than in just about any other investment.

Your Investment Choices

Let's see how stocks stack up to some of your other investment options:

Mutual Funds. Stock mutual funds can offer similar returns to investing in stocks on your own, but without all the extra work. When you invest in a fund, your money is pooled with that of other investors, and then it is managed by a group of professionals who try to earn a return by selecting stocks for the pool. (Shameless plug: We at Morningstar have a whole separate set of investing workbooks dedicated to mutual fund investing and finding the best funds.)

Beyond requiring much less effort, one key advantage of funds is that they can be less volatile. Simple statistics says that a portfolio is going to experience less volatility than the individual components of the portfolio. After all, individual stocks can and sometimes do go to zero, but if a mutual fund held 50 stocks, it would be very unlikely that all 50 of those stocks become worthless.

The flipside of this reduced volatility is that fund returns can be muted relative to individual stocks. In investing, risk and return are intimately correlated—reduce one, and odds are you will reduce the other. Another disadvantage to offloading all the effort of picking individual stocks is that you must pay someone else for this service. The professionals running mutual funds do not do so for free. They charge fees, and fees eat into returns.

Plus, the more money you have invested in mutual funds, the larger the absolute value of fees you will pay every year. For instance, paying 1% a year in fees on a $1,000 portfolio is not a big deal, but it's a much larger deal if the portfolio is worth $500,000. In the past, mutual funds often made the most sense for those with relatively small amounts to invest because they were the most cost-efficient. But with the advent of $10 (or less) per-trade commissions on stocks, this is no longer necessarily the case.

Just as picking the wrong stock is a risk, so is picking the wrong fund. What if the group of people you selected to manage your investment does not perform well? Just like stocks, there is no guarantee of a return in mutual funds.

It's also worth noting that investing in a mix of mutual funds and stocks can be a perfectly prudent strategy. Stocks versus funds (or any other investment vehicle) need not be an either/or proposition.

Pros and Cons of Stock Investing

Pros		Cons	
Pros	Potentially higher long-term returns.	Cons	Greater volatility.
	Full control of portfolio mix. You choose what you want to own.		Price to entry: the learning curve.
			Lots of ongoing work. (No pain, no gain.)
	Greater tax control.		
	If done right, lower trading costs & fees.		

Bonds. At their most basic, bonds are loans. When you buy a bond, you become a lender to an institution, and that institution pays you interest. As long as the institution does not go bankrupt, it will also pay back the principal on the bond, but no more than the principal.

There are two basic types of bonds: government bonds and corporate bonds. U.S. government bonds (otherwise known as T-bills or Treasuries) are issued and guaranteed by Uncle Sam. They typically offer a modest return with low risk. Corporate bonds are issued by companies and carry a higher degree of risk (should the company default) as well as return.

Bond investors must also consider interest rate risk. When prevailing interest rates rise, the market value of existing bonds tends to fall. (The opposite is also true.) The only way to alleviate interest rate risk is by holding the bond to maturity. Investing in corporate bonds also tends to require just as much homework as stock investing, yet bonds generally have lower returns.

Given their lower risk, there is certainly a place for bonds or bond mutual funds in most portfolios, but their relative safety comes with the price of lower expected returns compared with stocks over the long term.

Real Estate. Most people's homes are indeed their largest investments. We all have to live somewhere, and a happy side effect is that real estate tends to appreciate in value over time. But if you are going to use real estate as a true investment vehicle by buying a second home, a piece of land, or a rental property, it's important to keep the following in mind.

First, despite the exceptionally strong appreciation real estate values have had the past several years, real estate can and does occasionally decline in value. Second, real estate taxes will constantly eat into returns. Third, real estate owners must worry about physically maintaining their properties or must pay someone else to do it. Likewise, they often must deal with tenants and collect rents. Finally, real estate is rather illiquid and takes time to sell—a potential problem if you need your money back quickly.

Some people do nothing but invest their savings in real estate and do quite well. But just as stock investing requires effort, so does real estate investing.

Bank Savings Accounts. The problem with bank savings accounts and certificates of deposit is that they offer very low returns. The upside is that there is essentially zero risk in these investment vehicles, and your principal is protected. These types of accounts are fine as rainy-day funds—a place to park money for short-term spending needs or for an emergency. But they really should not be viewed as long-term investment vehicles.

The low returns of these investments are a problem because of inflation. For instance, if you get a 3% return on a savings account, but inflation is also dropping the buying power of your dollar by 3% a year, you really aren't making any money. Your real return (return adjusted for inflation) is zero, meaning that your money is not really working for you.

How Stocks Stack Up

	Stocks	Funds	Bonds	Real Estate	Savings Account
Returns	▪▪▪▪▪	▪▪▪▪▫	▪▪▪▫▫	▪▪▪▫▫	▪▫▫▫▫
Volatility	▪▪▪▪▪	▪▪▪▪▫	▪▪▫▫▫	▪▪▪▫▫	▪▫▫▫▫
Risk	▪▪▪▪▪	▪▪▪▪▫	▪▪▪▫▫	▪▪▪▫▫	▪▪▫▫▫
Liquidity	▪▪▪▪▫	▪▪▪▪▫	▪▪▪▪▫	▪▫▫▫▫	▪▪▪▪▫
Effort	▪▪▪▪▪	▪▪▪▫▫	▪▪▪▪▫	▪▪▪▪▫	▪▫▫▫▫
Cost & Fees	▪▪▫▫▫	▪▪▪▪▫	▪▪▪▪▫	▪▪▪▪▫	▪▪▫▫▫

The Bottom Line

Though investing in stocks may indeed require more work and carry a higher degree of risk compared with other investment opportunities, you cannot ignore the higher potential return that stocks provide. And as we will show in the next lesson, given enough time, a slightly higher return on your investments can lead to dramatically larger dollar sums for whatever your financial goals in life may be.

Investor's Checklist

▶ Investing in stocks is an intellectual exercise that requires effort, but it is an effort that can bear many fruits.

▶ Among the potential investments one can make, stocks provide the largest long-term returns, but they also have the largest volatility.

▶ Stocks are ownership interests in companies. They are not simply pieces of paper to be traded.

Quiz

Answers to this quiz can be found on page 165

1   Which of the following types of investments provide the largest long-term returns?

a	Stocks.
b	Bonds.
c	Savings accounts.

2   Which of the following types of investments are the most volatile in their pricing?

a	Stocks.
b	Bonds.
c	Savings accounts.

3   Which of the following skills sets is NOT needed to be a successful investor?

a	Discipline.
b	A critical eye.
c	Advanced statistics.

4   Over the long term, which type of investment provides the lowest real (inflation adjusted) returns?

a	Stocks.
b	Mutual funds.
c	Savings accounts.

5   When you buy a stock, you are:

a	Making a loan to a company.
b	Buying an ownership interest in a company.
c	Investing in the government.

Worksheet

1   Why do you want to invest at all? Write down your financial goals in life in the space below. The effort you put into these workbooks will certainly help you toward these goals.

Answers to this worksheet can be found on page 175

```
┌─────────────────────────┐  ┌─────────────────────────┐
│                         │  │                         │
└─────────────────────────┘  └─────────────────────────┘
┌─────────────────────────┐  ┌─────────────────────────┐
│                         │  │                         │
└─────────────────────────┘  └─────────────────────────┘
┌─────────────────────────┐  ┌─────────────────────────┐
│                         │  │                         │
└─────────────────────────┘  └─────────────────────────┘
```

2   What are some of the things that concern you about stock investing? Write them here. Are you willing to see the value of your investments continuously fluctuate (sometimes significantly) in order to receive a higher long-term return?

3   Can you describe what a stock actually is?

4   Write below some products and brands you like. Figure out which companies make these. Chances are you can become an owner in these businesses.

Product names	Company

11

Lesson 102: The Magic of Compounding

"When my mother used to sing me songs about compound interest, there wasn't any need to go any further."—Warren Buffett

When you were a kid, perhaps one of your friends asked you the following trick question: "Would you rather have $10,000 per day for 30 days or a penny that doubled in value every day for 30 days?" Today, we know to choose the doubling penny, because at the end of 30 days, we'd have about $5 million versus the $300,000 we'd have if we chose $10,000 per day.

Compound interest is often called the eighth wonder of the world because it seems to possess magical powers, like turning a penny into $5 million. The great part about compound interest is that it applies to money, and it helps us to achieve our financial goals, such as becoming a millionaire, retiring comfortably, or being financially independent.

The Components of Compound Interest

A dollar invested at a 10% return will be worth $1.10 in a year. Invest that $1.10 and get 10% again, and you'll end up with $1.21 two years from your original investment. The first year earned you only $0.10, but the second generated $0.11. This is compounding at its most basic level: gains begetting more gains. Increase the amounts and the time involved, and the benefits of compounding become much more pronounced.

In addition to a financial calculator, spreadsheet, or table of present values, the following Web sites will help you to calculate compound interest:

American Savings Education Council: Financial Calculators
www.choosetosave.org/tools/fincalcs.htm

Math.com: Saving/Compounding Calculator
www.math.com/students/calculators/source/compound.htm

Online Calculators

Compound interest can be calculated using the following formula:

$$FV = PV (1 + i)^N$$

FV = Future Value (the amount you will have in the future)
PV = Present Value (the amount you have today)
i = Interest (your rate of return or interest rate earned)
N = Number of Years (the length of time you invest)

Who Wants to Be a Millionaire?

As a fun way to learn about compound interest, let's examine a few different ways to become a millionaire. First we'll look at a couple of investors and how they have chosen to accumulate $1 million.

1. Jack saves $25,000 per year for 40 years.
2. Jeff starts with $1 and doubles his money each year for 20 years.

While most would love to be able to save $25,000 every year like Jack, this is too difficult for most of us. If we earn an average of $50,000 per year, we would have to save 50% of our salary!

In the second example, Jeff uses compound interest, invests only $1, and earns 100% on his money for 20 consecutive years. The magic of compound interest has made it easy for Jeff to earn his $1 million and to do it in only half the time as Jack. However, Jeff's example is also a little unrealistic since very few investments can earn 100% in any given year, much less for 20 consecutive years.

Rule of 72

A simple way to know the time it takes for money to double is to use the rule of 72. For example, if you wanted to know how many years it would take for an investment earning 12% to double, simply divide 72 by 12, and the answer would be approximately six years. The reverse is also true. If you wanted to know what interest rate you would have to earn to double your money in five years, then divide 72 by five, and the answer is about 15%.

Time Is on Your Side

Between these two extremes, there are realistic situations in which compound interest helps the average individual. One of the key concepts about compounding is this: The earlier you start, the better off you'll be. So what are you waiting for?

Let's consider the case of two other investors, Luke and Walt, who'd also like to become millionaires. Say Luke put $2,000 per year into the market between the ages of 24 and 30, that he earned a 12% aftertax return, and that he continued to earn 12% per year until he retired at age 65. Walt also put in $2,000 per year, earned the same return, but waited until he was 30 to start and continued to invest $2,000 per year until he retired at age 65. In the end, both would end up with about $1 million. However, Luke had to invest only $12,000 (i.e., $2,000 for six years), while Walt had to invest $72,000 ($2,000 for 36 years) or six times the amount that Walt invested, just for waiting only six years to start investing.

Why Investing Early Is Important

Walt	Age	Amount Invested in $	With 12% Interest	Luke	Age	Amount Invested in $	With 12% Interest
	24	—	—		24	2,000	2,240
	25	—	—		25	2,000	4,749
	26	—	—		26	2,000	7,559
	27	—	—		27	2,000	10,706
	28	—	—		28	2,000	14,230
	29	—	—		29	2,000	18,178
	30	2,000	2,240		30	—	20,359
	35	2,000	18,178		35	—	35,880
	40	2,000	46,266		40	—	63,233
	45	2,000	95,767		45	—	111,438
	50	2,000	183,005		50	—	196,393
	55	2,000	336,748		55	—	346,111
	60	2,000	607,695		60	—	609,966
	65	2,000	1,085,197		65	—	1,074,968
	total amount invested	$72,000			total amount invested	$12,000	

Clearly, investing early can be at least as important as the actual amount invested over a lifetime. Therefore, to truly benefit from the magic of compounding, it's important to start investing early. We can't stress this fact enough! After all, it's not just how much money you start with that counts, it's also how much time you allow that money to work for you.

In our first example, Jack had to save $25,000 a year for 40 years to reach $1 million without the benefit of compound interest. Luke and Walt, however, were each able to become millionaires by saving only $12,000 and $72,000, respectively, in relatively modest $2,000 increments. Luke and Walt earned $988,000 and $928,000, respectively, due to compound interest. Gains beget gains, which beget even larger gains. This is again the magic of compound interest.

Last Is Certainly Not Least

Interestingly, if you start with $1 and double your money every year for 20 years, it's the last year that's most powerful. After the 19th doubling, you'd have only about $500,000. So, although compound interest is magical, patience is the real virtue.

Why Is Compound Interest Important to Stock Investing?

In addition to the amount you invest and an early start, the rate of return you earn from investing is also crucial. The higher the rate, the more money you'll have later. Let's assume that Luke from our previous example had two sisters who, at age 24, also began saving $2,000 a year for six years. But unlike Luke, who earned 12%, sister Charlotte earned only 8%, while sister Rose did not make good investment decisions and earned only 4%. When they all retired at age 65, Luke would have $1,074,968, Charlotte would have $253,025, and Rose would have only $56,620. Even though Luke earned only 8 percentage points more per year on his investments, or $160 per year more on the initial $2,000 investment, he would end up with about 20 times more money than Rose.

Why Return Matters

In the table below we check in on Luke and his sisters, Rose and Charlotte, from age 24 to 30 and every five years after that until retirement, at age 65.

Age	Amount Invested in $	Rose 4% Rate of Return	Charlotte 8% Rate of Return	Luke 12% Rate of Return
24	2,000	2,080	2,160	2,240
25	2,000	4,243	4,493	4,749
26	2,000	6,493	7,012	7,559
27	2,000	8,833	9,733	10,706
28	2,000	11,266	12,672	14,230
29	2,000	13,797	15,846	18,178
30	—	14,348	17,113	20,359
35	—	17,457	25,145	35,880
40	—	21,239	36,946	63,233
45	—	25,841	54,286	111,438
50	—	31,439	79,764	196,393
55	—	38,251	117,200	346,111
60	—	46,538	172,205	609,966
65	—	56,620	253,025	1,074,968
total amount invested	$12,000			

Clearly, a few percentage points in investment returns or interest rates can mean a huge difference in your future wealth. Therefore, while stocks may be a riskier investment in the short run, in the long run the rewards can certainly outweigh the risks.

The Bottom Line

Compound interest can help you attain your goals in life. In order to use it most effectively, you should start investing early, invest as much as possible, and attempt to earn a reasonable rate of return.

Investor's Checklist

▶ The three components that determine how much money you will have in the future are: the amount of money invested, the length of time invested, and the rate of return. The earlier you invest, the more you invest, and the higher the rate of return, the more money you'll have in the future.

▶ The formula for compound interest is $FV = PV (1 + i)^N$. You can use a business calculator or a financial calculator on the Internet to easily figure out what is needed to achieve your financial goals.

▶ The rule of 72 is an easy rule of thumb that tells you how often your money doubles. Divide 72 by the percentage rate of return to determine the number of years required for your money to double at that rate of return.

▶ With compound interest, the last few years of compounding make the most difference.

▶ The primary attraction to investing in stocks is that the long-run rate of return is higher than the interest earned in bank accounts or bonds.

Quiz

1 Using the rule of 72, an investment earning 10% per year would double in approximately how many years?

a	10.
b	7.
c	5.

Answers to this quiz can be found on page 165

2 Using the rule of 72, if you invested $10,000 at 12% per year, in 12 years, you would have how much money?

a	$20,000
b	$30,000
c	$40,000

3 Which of the following is not a component of compound interest?

a	Time.
b	Interest rate.
c	Financial calculator.

4 If you had invested $1 and doubled your investment 20 years in a row, you would have $1 million dollars. In the last year (year 20), you would have made how much money?

a	$100,00
b	$50,000
c	$500,000

5 Which of the following is not true?

a	The earlier you invest, the more money you'll have in the future.
b	The lower the interest rate, the more money you'll have in the future.
c	The longer you invest, the more money you'll have in the future.

Worksheet

Answers to this worksheet can be found on page 175

1   In the column on the left-hand side, write down your current age. Then for each successive box, add six years. Therefore, if you are 30, you'll have listed 30, 36, 42, etc. To the right of your first age box write down $30,000.

Using the rule of 72, assume you are a superstar investor and can double your investments every six years through a 12% rate of return. Therefore, if you are 30, at age 36 you'd write $60,000 and keep on doubling the amount for each age at each successive box. Vary your initial investment amount to your circumstance and continue doubling your investments as long as you wish.

How much money do you have at your planned retirement age? Are you surprised? Why isn't everyone a millionaire?

Age	Money	Age	Money

2   Using an Internet Web site or a financial calculator, determine two different ways you could become a millionaire. For example, Luke became a millionaire by investing $2,000 per year for six years beginning at age 24 and earning 12% annually until age 65.

1.

2.

3   Of the three components of compound interest, which can you control when investing, if any, and why?

Lesson 103: Investing for the Long Run

"I have but one lamp by which my feet are guided, and that is the lamp of experience. I know of no way of judging the future but by the past."—*Patrick Henry*

In the last lesson, we noticed that the difference of only a few percentage points in investment returns or interest rates can have a huge impact on your future wealth. Therefore, in the long run, the rewards of investing in stocks can outweigh the risks. We'll examine this risk/reward dynamic in this lesson.

Volatility of Single Stocks

Individual stocks tend to have highly volatile prices, and the returns you might receive on any single stock may vary wildly. If you invest in the right stock, you could make bundles of money. For instance, Eaton Vance, an investment-management company, has had the best-performing stock for the last 25 years. If you had invested $10,000 in 1979 in Eaton Vance, assuming you had reinvested all dividends, your investment would have been worth $10.6 million by December 2004.

On the downside, since the returns on stock investments are not guaranteed, you risk losing everything on any given investment. There are hundreds of recent examples of dot-com investments that went bankrupt or are trading for a fraction of their former highs. Even established, well-known companies such as Enron, WorldCom, and Kmart filed for bankruptcy, and investors in these companies lost everything.

Between these two extremes is the daily, weekly, monthly, and yearly fluctuation of any given company's stock price. Most stocks won't double in the coming year, nor will many go to zero. But do consider that the average difference between the yearly high and low stock prices of the typical stock on the New York Stock Exchange is nearly 40%.

In addition to being volatile, there is the risk that a single company's stock price may not increase significantly over time. In 1965, you could have purchased General Motors' stock for $50 per share (split adjusted). In the following decades, though, this investment has only spun its wheels. By May 2005, your shares of General Motors would be worth only about $30 each. Though dividends would have provided some ease to the pain, General Motors' return has been terrible. You would have been better off if you had invested your money in a bank savings account instead of General Motors' stock.

Tale of Two Returns: General Motors Versus Eaton Vance

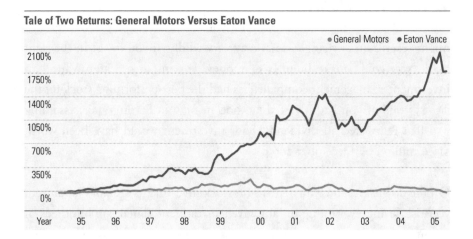

Clearly, if you put all of your eggs in a single basket, sometimes that basket may fail, breaking all the eggs. Other times, that basket will hold the equivalent of a winning lottery ticket.

The Stock Market Crash of 1929	The biggest stock market crash in the United States during the 20th century occurred in 1929. In reality, the 1929 crash should really be referred to as the stock market crash of 1929 to 1932. While the market fell by 17% for the year in 1929, the market declined an incredible 89% from the high in 1929 to the low of 1932. The largest one-day crash occurred on Monday, Oct. 19, 1987, when the Dow Jones Industrial Average declined 22%.

Volatility of the Stock Market

One way of reducing the risk of investing in individual stocks is by holding a larger number of stocks in a portfolio. However, even a portfolio of stocks containing a wide variety of companies can fluctuate wildly. You may experience large losses over short periods. Market dips, sometimes significant, are simply part of investing in stocks.

For example, consider the Dow Jones Industrials Index, a basket of 30 of the most popular, and some of the best, companies in America. (For more information on the S&P 500 and the Dow Jones Industrial Average, see Lesson 111.) If during the last 100 years you had held an investment tracking the Dow, there would have been 10 different occasions when that investment would have lost 40% or more of its value.

Annual Returns Over the Years

	Simple Annual Returns									
	'00	'01	'02	'03	'04	'05	'06	'07	'08	'09
1900	7%	-9%	0%	-24%	42%	38%	-2%	-38%	47%	15%
1910	-18%	0%	8%	-10%	-31%	82%	-4%	-22%	11%	30%
1920	-33%	13%	22%	-3%	26%	30%	0%	29%	48%	-17%
1930	-34%	-53%	-23%	67%	4%	39%	25%	-33%	28%	-3%
1940	-13%	-15%	8%	14%	12%	27%	-8%	2%	-2%	13%
1950	18%	14%	8%	-4%	44%	21%	2%	-13%	34%	16%
1960	-9%	19%	-11%	17%	15%	11%	-19%	15%	4%	-15%
1970	5%	6%	15%	-17%	-28%	38%	18%	-17%	-3%	4%
1980	15%	-9%	20%	20%	-4%	28%	23%	2%	12%	27%
1990	-4%	20%	4%	14%	2%	33%	26%	23%	16%	25%
2000	-6%	-7%	-17%							

Copyright 2003, Crestmont Research (www.CrestmontResearch.com).

As shown in the preceding chart, the yearly returns in the stock market also fluctuate dramatically. The highest one-year rate of return of 67% occurred in 1933, while the lowest one-year rate of return of negative 53% occurred in 1931. It should be obvious by now that stocks are volatile, and there is a significant risk if you cannot ride out market losses in the short term. But don't worry; there is a bright side to this story.

Over the Long Term, Stocks Are Best

Despite all the short-term risks and volatility, stocks as a group have had the highest long-term returns of any investment type. This is an incredibly important fact! When the stock market has crashed, the market has always rebounded and gone on to new highs. Stocks have outperformed bonds on a total real return (after inflation) basis, on average. This holds true even after market peaks.

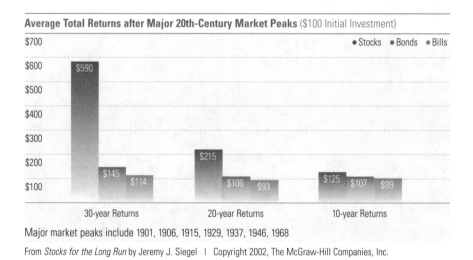

Average Total Returns after Major 20th-Century Market Peaks ($100 Initial Investment)

Major market peaks include 1901, 1906, 1915, 1929, 1937, 1946, 1968

From *Stocks for the Long Run* by Jeremy J. Siegel | Copyright 2002, The McGraw-Hill Companies, Inc.

As shown in the chart above, if you had deplorable timing and invested $100 into the stock market during any of the seven major market peaks in the 20th century, that investment, over the next 10 years, would have been worth $125 after inflation, but it would have been worth only $107 had you invested in bonds, and $99 if you had purchased government Treasury bills. In other words, stocks have been the best-performing asset class over the long term, while government bonds, in these cases, merely kept up with inflation.

This is the whole reason to go through the effort of investing in stocks. Again, even if you had invested in stocks at the highest peak in the market, your total after-inflation returns after 10 years would have been higher for stocks than either bonds or cash. Had you invested a little at a time, not just when stocks were expensive but also when they were cheap, your returns would have been much greater.

Time Is on Your Side

Just as compound interest can dramatically grow your wealth over time, the longer you invest in stocks, the better off you will be. With time, your chances of making money increase, and the volatility of your returns decreases.

The average annual return for the S&P 500 stock index for a single year has ranged from negative 39% to positive 61%, while averaging 13.2%. After holding stocks for five years, average annualized returns have ranged from negative 4% to positive 30%, while averaging 11.9%. Finally, if your holding period is 20 years, you never lost money, with 20-year returns ranging from positive 6.4% to positive 15%, with the average being 9.5%.

These returns easily surpass those you can get from any of the other major types of investments. Again, as your holding period increases, the expected return variation decreases, and the likelihood for a positive return increases. (See chart on next page.) This is why it is important to have a long-term investment horizon when getting started in stocks.

Average Annual Returns of U.S. Stocks for Different Holding Periods

The longer you invest, the lower the volatility of your returns.

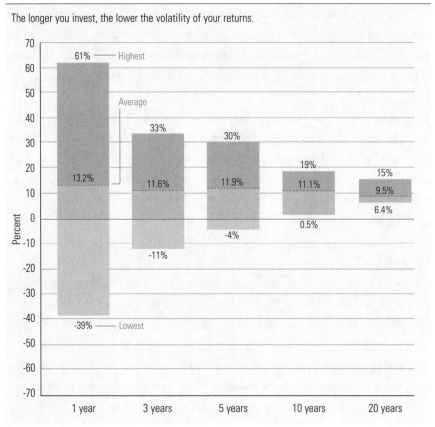

From *Investing for Dummies*

Why Stocks Perform the Best

While historical results certainly offer insight into the types of returns to expect in the future, it is still important to ask the following questions: Why, exactly, have stocks been the best-performing asset class? And why should we expect those types of returns to continue? In other words, why should we expect history to repeat?

Quite simply, stocks allow investors to own companies that have the ability to create enormous economic value. Stock investors have full exposure to this upside. For instance, in 1985, would you have rather lent Microsoft money at a 6% interest rate, or would you have rather been an owner, seeing the value of your investment grow several-hundred fold?

Because of the risk, stock investors also require the largest return compared with other types of investors before they will give their money to companies to grow their businesses. More often than not, companies are able to generate enough value to cover this return demanded by their owners.

Though stocks typically perform best over the long term, there can be extended periods of poor performance. For example, the Dow Jones Industrial Average peaked in 1966 and didn't surpass its old high again until 16 years later in 1982. But the following 20 years were great for stocks, with the Dow increasing more than tenfold by 2002.	**The Worst of Times…** **The Best of Times**

Meanwhile, bond investors do not reap the benefit of economic expansion to nearly as large a degree. When you buy a bond, the interest rate on the original investment will never increase. Your theoretical loan to Microsoft yielding 6% would have never yielded more than 6%, no matter how well the company did. Being an owner certainly exposes you to greater risk and volatility, but the sky is also the limit on the potential return.

The Bottom Line

While stocks make an attractive investment in the long run, stock returns are not guaranteed and tend to be volatile in the short term. Therefore, we do not recommend that you invest in stocks to achieve your short-term goals. To be effective, you should invest in stocks only to meet long-term objectives that are at least five years away. And the longer you invest, the greater your chances of achieving the types of returns that make investing in stocks worthwhile.

Investor's Checklist

► Stock returns are not guaranteed. While stock market returns over a five-year period have averaged about 12% annually, the stock market can also decline for several years in a row.

► The worst fall in the stock market was between 1929 and 1932 when the market declined by 89%. There have been about 10 periods in the last century when the stock market has plunged by more than 40%.

► Individual stocks are volatile. The difference between the yearly high and low price for the typical stock on the New York Stock Exchange is near 40%.

► The longer you invest in stocks, the greater the chances you will make money. In any 20-year period over the last 200 years, stocks have returned a positive real (after inflation) rate of return.

► Even if you had invested in stocks at only the highest peaks in the market, your total real returns after 10 years would have been higher for stocks than either bonds or cash.

Quiz

1   The average yearly difference between the high and low of the typical stock is between:

a	30% and 50%.
b	10% and 30%.
c	50% and 70%.

Answers to this quiz can be found on page 166

2   If you were saving to buy a car in three years, what percentage of your savings for the car should you invest in the stock market?

a	50%.
b	70%.
c	0%.

3   If you were investing for your retirement, which is more than 10 years away, based on historical returns in the 20th century, what percentage of the time would you have been better off by investing only in stocks versus a combination of stocks, bonds, and cash?

a	50%.
b	100%.
c	0%.

4   Well-known stocks like General Motors:

a	Always outperform the stock market.
b	Are too highly priced for the average investor.
c	Can underperform the stock market.

5   Which of the following is true:

a	After adjusting for inflation, bonds outperform stocks.
b	When you invest in stocks, you will earn 12% interest on your money.
c	Stock investments should be part of your long-term investment portfolio.

Worksheet

Answers to this worksheet can be found on page 176

1   Assuming you had to save money for a down payment on your car, would you invest in the stock market? How would your answer change if you had to invest for your retirement?

2   Janet has recently graduated from college and would like to start saving to become financially independent by age 55. She wants to invest 100% of her money in stocks. What would you advise her to do?

3   Write down your financial goals in life and the amount of time in years before you expect to reach those goals. If you are going to invest in stocks to achieve these goals, are the goals far enough out to minimize the risk of short-term volatility wiping out your returns? Are you willing to hold on through the dips your investment portfolio will inevitably experience in order to benefit from the long-term returns of stocks?

Goal	Time (Years)	Far enough out for stocks?
		◯ Yes ◯ No
		◯ Yes ◯ No
		◯ Yes ◯ No

4   Write down the kind of returns you expect by investing in stocks over the next year. What about the next 10 years? Are these expectations consistent with what stocks have returned historically?

Lesson 104: What Matters and What Doesn't

"The gambling known as business looks with austere disfavor upon the business known as gambling."—Ambrose Bierce

Different people have different notions of what stock investing is all about. Before we go any further in this workbook series, we want to put things into focus and set you on the right path.

Investing Does Not Equal Trading

Your perception of stock investing may involve highly caffeinated, frantic traders sweating in front of a half dozen computer screens packed with information, while phones ring off the hook in the background.

Feel free to dump these images from your mind because solid stock investing is not about trading, having the fastest computers, or getting the most up-to-the-second information. Though some professionals make their living by creating a liquid market for stocks, actively "day trading" is simply not how most good investing is done by individuals.

Beyond having to expend an incredible amount of effort to track stocks on an hour-by-hour basis, active day traders have three powerful factors working against them. First, trading commissions can rack up quickly, dramatically eroding returns. Second, there are other trading costs in terms of the bid/ask spread, or the small spread between what buyers are bidding and sellers are asking at any moment. These more hidden frictional costs are typically only a small fraction of the stock price, but they can add up to big bucks if incurred often enough. Finally, frequent traders tend not to be tax efficient, and paying more taxes can greatly diminish returns.

Just as someone can be a great racecar driver without being a mechanical engineer, you can be a great investor without having a clue about how the trades actually get executed in the market. How your orders flow from one computer system to the other is of little consequence.

Just remember that investing is like a chess game, where thought, patience, and the ability to peer into the future are rewarded. Making the right moves is much more important than moving quickly.

Investing Means Owning Businesses

If the mechanics of actual trading mean little, what does matter? Do charts of stock prices hold the answers? We've said it once, and we'll say it again and again: When you buy stocks, you are buying ownership interests in companies. Stocks are not just pieces of paper to be traded.

So if you are buying businesses, it makes sense to think like a business owner. This means learning how to read financial statements, considering how companies actually make money, spotting trends, and figuring out which businesses have the best competitive positions. It also means coming up with appropriate prices to pay for the businesses you want to buy. Notice that none of this requires lightning-fast reflexes!

You should also buy stocks like you would any other large purchase: with lots of research, care, and the intention to hold as long as it makes sense. Some people will spend an entire weekend driving around to different stores to save $60 on a television, but they put hardly any thought into the thousands of dollars they could create for themselves by purchasing the right stocks (or avoiding the wrong ones). Again, investing is an intellectual exercise, but one that can have a large payoff.

You Buy Stocks, Not the Market

We've all seen the prognosticators on television, predicting where the market is going to go in the future. One thing to remember when listening to these market premonitions is that stock investing is about buying individual stocks, not the market as a whole. If you pick the right stocks, you can make money no matter what the broader market does.

Another reason to heavily discount what the prognosticators say is that correctly predicting market movements is nearly impossible. No one has done it consistently and accurately. There are simply too many moving parts, and too many unknowns. By limiting the field to individual businesses of interest, you can focus on what you can actually own while dramatically cutting down on the unknowns. You can save a lot of energy by simply tuning out market predictions.

We established in the previous lesson that stocks are volatile. Why is that? Does the value of any given business really change up to 50% year-to-year? (Imagine the chaos if the value of our homes changed this much!) The fact is, "Mr. Market" tends to be a bit of an extremist in the short term, overreacting to both good and bad news. We will talk more about this phenomenon later, but it is nevertheless a good fact to know when starting.

	A Broken Clock
With so many predictions about the stock market floating around, simple statistics says there are bound to be a handful of them that come true. When thinking about this, it is helpful to remember the saying: "A broken clock is correct twice a day."	

Competitive Positioning Is Most Important

Future profits drive stock prices over the long term, so it makes sense to focus on how a business is going to generate those future earnings. At Morningstar, we believe competitive positioning, or the ability of a business to keep competitors at bay, is the most important determining factor of future profits.

Despite where the financial media may spend most of its energy, competitive positioning is more important than the economic outlook, more important than the near-term flow of news that jostles stock prices, and even more important than management quality at a company.

It may be helpful to think of the investing process as if you were planning a trip across the ocean. You cannot do anything about the current weather or the tides (the current economic conditions). You can try to wait out bad weather that might sink your ship, but then you are also giving up time. And as we showed in Lesson 102, time is a precious resource in investing.

The main thing you can control is what ship to board. Think of the seaworthiness of a ship as the competitive positioning of a business, and the horsepower of the engine as its cash flow. Some ships have thick, reinforced metal hulls, while others have rotting wood. Clearly, you would pick the ships that are the most seaworthy (with the best competitive positioning) and have the most horsepower (cash flow).

Though the ship's captain (company management) certainly matters, the quality of the ship is more important. On a solid vessel, as long as the captain does not mess up, there is not much difference between a good and a great captain. Meanwhile, there is nothing the best skipper can do if the boat's engine is broken and the boat is constantly taking on water (poor business). To relate this to stocks, business economics trump management skill.

It's also worth noting that all ships will experience waves (volatility). And though it is true that a rising tide lifts all ships, the tides have nothing to do with the quality of the boats on the sea. All else equal, a better ship is still going to arrive faster, and a company with the best competitive positioning is going to create the most value for its shareholders. We will talk about exactly how to spot the best ships later in this book (Lesson 112) as well as throughout the second workbook in this series.

The Bottom Line

It is very easy for new stock investors to get started on the wrong track by focusing only on the mechanics of trading or the overall direction of the market. To get yourself in the proper mind-set, tune out the noise and focus on studying individual businesses and their ability to create future profits. In the coming lessons, we will begin to build the skills you will need to become a successful buyer of businesses.

Investor's Checklist

▶ Active traders have three things working against them: the bid/ask spread, commissions, and taxes.

▶ Stocks are not just pieces of paper to be traded; they are pieces of businesses.

▶ The stock market as a whole is nearly impossible to predict, but predicting the outcome of individual businesses is a more manageable exercise.

▶ Mr. Market is highly temperamental, over-reacting to both good and bad news.

▶ Future profits drive stock prices over the long term, and the competitive positioning of a business is the most important factor in its ability to generate future earnings.

Quiz

Answers to this quiz can be found on page 166

1   In general, the more frequently you trade:

a	The higher your expected return from stock investing.
b	The less you will pay in total trading commissions.
c	The higher your tax bill.

2   The stock market tends to:

a	Be temperamental, over-reacting to near-term news.
b	Be perfectly efficient, always valuing future cash flow accurately.
c	Move with the phases of the moon.

3   What will drive the price of a company's stock the most over the long term?

a	Economic conditions over the next year.
b	The future profits and cash flow a company can generate.
c	The education level of top management.

4   To be a successful stock investor, you need:

a	To be able to think quickly, with fast reflexes.
b	A powerful computer with up-to-the-minute information.
c	Patience and the ability to think about future trends.

5   What should you pay the most attention to?

a	Charts of stock prices.
b	A company's competitive positioning.
c	The predicted movement of the overall stock market.

Worksheet

1 Before reading this lesson, what were your impressions about stocks and the people investing in them? What kind of skills did you think you needed? What are your impressions now?

Answers to this worksheet can be found on page 177

2 Write down the three forces that frequent traders have to work against. How does taking a long-term investing approach minimize these costs?

1.

2.

3.

3 Can you name some investment approaches you've seen promoted that do not make any sense to you? (Example: Using astrology to pick stocks.)

4 Where do you think the Dow Jones Industrial Average will be next month? Next year? Why?

Digging into a Company

Lesson 105: The Purpose of a Company

"The chief business of the American people is business."—Calvin Coolidge

It's worth repeating that when you hold a stock, you own part of a company. Part of being an owner is understanding the financial underpinnings of any given business, and this lesson will provide an introduction.

The main purpose of a company is to take money from investors (their creditors and shareholders) and generate profits on their investments. Creditors and shareholders carry different risks with their investments, and thus they have different return opportunities. Creditors bear less risk and receive a fixed return regardless of a company's performance (unless the firm defaults). Shareholders carry all the risks of ownership, and their return depends on a company's underlying business performance. When companies generate lots of profits, shareholders stand to benefit the most.

As we learned in Lesson 101, at the end of the day, investors have many choices about where to put their money; they can invest it into savings accounts, government bonds, stocks, or other investment vehicles. In each, investors expect a return on their investment. Stocks represent ownership interests in companies that are expected to create value with the money that is invested in them by their owners.

Money In and Money Out

Companies need money to operate and grow their businesses in order to generate returns for their investors. Investors put money—called capital—into a company, and then it is the company's responsibility to create additional money—called profits—for investors. The ratio of the profit to the capital is called the return on capital. It is important to remember that the absolute level of profits in dollar terms is less important than profit as a percentage of the capital invested.

For example, a company may make $1 billion in profits for a given year, but it may have taken $20 billion worth of capital to do so, creating a meager 5% return on capital. This particular company is not very profitable. Another firm may generate just $100 million in profits but only need $500 million to do so, boasting a 20% return on capital. This company is highly profitable. A return on capital of 20% means that for every $1.00 that investors put into the company, the company earns $0.20 per year.

The Two Types of Capital

Before discussing return on capital further, it is important to distinguish between the two types of capital. As we mentioned above, two types of investors invest capital into companies: creditors ("loaners") and shareholders ("owners"). Creditors provide a company with debt capital, and shareholders provide a company with equity capital.

Creditors are typically banks, bondholders, and suppliers. They lend money to companies in exchange for a fixed return on their debt capital, usually in the form of interest payments. Companies also agree to pay back the principal on their loans.

The interest rate will be higher than the interest rate of government bonds because companies generally have a higher risk of defaulting on their interest payments and principal. Lenders generally require a return on their loans that is commensurate with the risks associated with the individual company. Therefore, a steady company will borrow money cheaply (lower interest payments), but a risky business will have to pay more (higher interest payments).

Shareholders that supply companies with equity capital are typically banks, mutual or hedge funds, and private investors. They give money to a company in exchange for an ownership interest in that business. Unlike creditors, shareholders do not get a fixed return on their investment because they are part owners of the company. When a company sells shares to the public (in other words, "goes public" to be "publicly traded"), it is actually selling an ownership stake in itself and not a promise to pay a fixed amount each year.

Shareholders are entitled to the profits, if any, generated by the company after everyone else—employees, vendors, lenders—gets paid. The more shares you own, the greater your claim on these profits and potential dividends. Owners have potentially unlimited upside profits, but they could also lose their entire investment if the company fails.

It is also important to keep in mind a company's total number of shares outstanding at any given time. Shareholders can benefit more from owning one share of a billion-dollar company that has only 100 shares (a 1% ownership interest) than by owning 100 shares of a billion-dollar company that has a million shares outstanding (a 0.01% ownership interest).

Once a Profit Is Created...

Companies usually pay out their profits in the form of dividends, or they reinvest the money back into the business. Dividends provide shareholders with a cash payment, and reinvested earnings offer shareholders the chance to receive more profits from the underlying business in the future. Many companies, especially young ones, pay no dividends. Any profits they make are plowed back into their businesses.

Always keep track of what your company does with its profits. As a shareholder with an interest in the company, you want to make sure that profits are reinvested in a way that maximizes your return.

Follow the Money

One of the most important jobs of any company's management is to decide whether to pay out profits as dividends or to reinvest the money back into the business. Companies that care about shareholders will reinvest the money only if they have promising opportunities to invest in—opportunities that should earn a higher return than shareholders could get on their own.

Different Capital, Different Risk, Different Return

Debt and equity capital each have different risk profiles. Therefore, as we showed in Lesson 103, each type of capital offers investors different return opportunities. Creditors shoulder less risk than shareholders because they are accepting a lower rate of return on the debt capital they supply to a company. When a company pays out the profits generated each year, creditors are paid before anyone else. Creditors can break up a company if it does not have sufficient money to cover its interest payments, and they wield a big stick.

Consequently, companies understand that there is a big difference between borrowing money from creditors and raising money from shareholders. If a firm is unable to pay the interest on a corporate bond or the principal when it comes due, the company is bankrupt. The creditors can then come in and divvy up the firm's assets in order to recover whatever they can from their investments. Any assets left over after the creditors are done belong to shareholders, but often such leftovers do not amount to much, if anything at all.

Shareholders take on more risk than creditors because they only get the profits left over after everyone else gets paid. If nothing is left over, they receive nothing in return. They are the "residual" claimants to a company's profits. However, there is an important trade-off. If a company generates lots of profits, shareholders enjoy the highest returns. The sky is the limit for owners and their profits. Meanwhile, loaners keep receiving the same interest payment year in and year out, regardless of how high the company's profits may reach. By contrast, owners keep whatever profits are left over. And the more that is left over, the higher their return on capital.

Vote!	Each share of a company provides its holder with voting rights to elect a company's board of directors. Shareholders can also vote on important company decisions such as merger and acquisition offers. The more shares you own, the greater your voting power. Be sure to cast your vote on all important company matters because it is a fundamental benefit of your ownership stake in a company.

Return on Capital and Return on Stock

The market often takes a long time to reward shareholders with a return on stock that corresponds to a company's return on capital. To better understand this statement, it is crucial to separate return on capital from return on stock. Return on capital is a measure of a company's profitability, but return on stock represents a combination of dividends and increases in the stock price (better known as capital gains). The two simple formulas below outline the return calculations in more detail:

Return on Capital: $\dfrac{\text{Profit}}{\text{Invested Capital}}$

Return on Stock: Shareholder Total Return $\ominus$ Capital Gains $\oplus$ Dividends

The market frequently forgets the important relationship between return on capital and return on stock. A company can earn a high return on capital, but shareholders could still suffer if the market price of the stock decreases over the same period. Similarly, a terrible company with a low return on capital may see its stock price increase if the firm performed less terribly than the market had expected. Or maybe the company is currently losing lots of money, but investors have bid up its stock in anticipation of future profits.

In other words, in the short term, there can be a disconnect between how a company performs and how its stock performs. This is because a stock's market price is a function of the market's perception of the value of the future profits a company can create. Sometimes this perception is spot on; sometimes it is way off the mark. But over a longer period of time, the market tends to get it right, and the performance of a company's stock will mirror the performance of the underlying business.

The Voting and Weighing Machines

The father of value investing, Benjamin Graham, explained this concept by saying that in the short run, the market is like a voting machine—tallying up which firms are popular and unpopular. But in the long run, the market is like a weighing machine—assessing the substance of a company. The message is clear: What matters in the long run is a company's actual underlying business performance and not the investing public's fickle opinion about its prospects in the short run.

Over the long term, when companies perform well, their shares will do so, too. And when a company's business suffers, the stock will also suffer. For example, Starbucks has had phenomenal success at turning coffee—a simple product that used to be practically given away—into a premium product that people are willing to pay up for. Starbucks has enjoyed handsome growth in number of stores, profits, and share price. Starbucks also has a respectable return on capital of near 11% today.

Meanwhile, Sears has languished. It has had a difficult time competing with discount stores and strip malls, and it has not enjoyed any meaningful profit growth in years. Plus, its return on capital rarely tops 5%. As a result, its stock has bounced around without really going anywhere in decades.

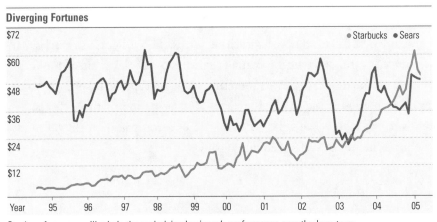

Diverging Fortunes

Stock performance will mimic the underlying business's performance over the long term.

The Bottom Line

In the end, stocks are ownership interests in companies. We can't emphasize this fact enough. Being a stockholder is being a partial owner of a company.

Over the long term, a company's business performance and its stock price will converge. The market rewards companies that earn high returns on capital over a long period. Companies that earn low returns may get an occasional bounce in the short term, but their long-term performance will be just as miserable as their returns on capital. The wealth a company creates—as measured by returns on capital—will find its way to shareholders over the long term in the form of dividends or stock appreciation.

Investor's Checklist
▶ A stock represents an ownership interest in a company, and the purpose of a company is to generate returns on the money invested by shareholders.
▶ Companies take money (capital) in from investors and are responsible for churning money (profits) out. The ratio of profit to capital is the return on capital.
▶ Debt and equity are the two types of capital invested into companies. Each type of capital has benefits and risks associated with it.
▶ Return on capital and return on stock are two different measures of a company's performance, but over time the two metrics will converge.
▶ Over the long term, when a company does well, your interest in that company will also do well.

Quiz

Answers to this quiz can be found on page 167

1   Which of the following best defines a stock?

a	A stock is a vehicle for speculative trading.
b	A stock is an ownership interest in a company.
c	A stock is a way to lend companies money.

2   What is the purpose of a company?

a	To take money from investors and spend it on lavish corporate expenses.
b	To make investors rich in the fastest way possible.
c	To take money from investors and generate profits on their investments.

3   Which of the following is a benefit of a bondholder over a stockholder?

a	If a company goes bankrupt, bondholders get paid before stockholders.
b	Bonds yield a higher return than stocks when a company does well.
c	If a company can't pay the interest on a corporate bond, the government will pay it.

4   Company A generates $500 million in profits and its return on capital is 10%. Company B generates $250 million in profits and its return on capital is 20%. Which company is more profitable?

a	Company A.
b	Company B.
c	Company A and Company B are equally profitable.

5   All else equal, if a company's total number of shares outstanding is increasing, your ownership stake in that company is:

a	Increasing.
b	Decreasing.
c	Remaining constant.

Worksheet

1   Explain some of the advantages and disadvantages of being a stockholder.

Answers to this worksheet can be found on page 177

Advantages:

Disadvantages:

2   Why do debt capital and equity capital offer different return opportunities?

3   Discuss the difference between return on capital and return on stock.

4   Would you prefer a company that in the past year has had a high return on capital or a high return on stock?

Lesson 106: Gathering Relevant Information

"Knowledge is of two kinds. We know a subject ourselves, or we know where we can find information on it."—Samuel Johnson

Now that you know the definition of a stock and the purpose of a company, how do you go about finding more information about a firm you may be interested in? Because knowledge truly is power when it comes to investing, your success as a stock investor depends on your ability to locate information and determine its importance. In this lesson, we'll point you in the right direction and tell you where to concentrate your efforts.

Sorting Out the Public Filings

At first, public filings may look like alphabet soup, but when researching a company, they are some of the most important documents you will read.

If a company has a stock on a major exchange like the New York Stock Exchange (NYSE), it is required to file certain documents for public consumption with the Securities and Exchange Commission (SEC). The SEC imposes guidelines on what information gets published in these filings, so they are somewhat uniform. Finally, companies are required to file documents in a timely fashion.

Among the public filings available, the most comprehensive and useful document is the 10-K. The 10-K is an annual report that outlines a wealth of general information about a company, including number of employees, business risks, description of properties, and strategies. The 10-K also contains the company's audited year-end financial statements. In addition to possessing crucial facts and figures, the 10-K also includes management's discussion and analysis of the past business year and compares it with preceding years.

We suggest making the 10-K the first stop in your journey to researching a company. How do you find a firm's 10-K? Just visit the SEC Web site (www.sec.gov), click on "Filings & Forms," and then "Search for Company Filings." After plugging your company's name into the "Companies & Other Filers" search, you can pick the 10-K out of the list of forms. Morningstar's Web site also has links directly to the SEC Web site. Just enter a company's name or ticker into the search box, and choose the "SEC Filings" link on the left.

What about all those other forms? Some of them are worth a read. For instance, the 10-Q contains some of the same data that you'll find in the 10-K, except that it is published on a quarterly basis. Although it's a little less comprehensive and the financial statements are typically unaudited, the 10-Q is a good way to keep tabs on a company throughout the year.

Why Do We Have the SEC and Public Filings?

The Securities and Exchange Commission was created after the 1929 crash greatly reduced the public's trust in the stock market. At the height of the depression that followed the crash, Congress passed two sets of laws, known as the Securities Act of 1933 and the Securities Exchange Act of 1934, that created the SEC and still provide the framework for securities regulation in the U.S. today. These acts are designed to promote stability in the markets and protect investors. As a result of these laws, companies are required to tell the truth about their businesses, and disclose the risks their owners face.

Another important document is the annual proxy statement, also called DEF 14A. In the proxy, you will find detailed information about executive compensation, the Board of directors, and the shareholder voting process. The proxy is a must-read for gaining better insight into the corporate governance of the company you're researching and determining your rights as a potential shareholder.

If you're interested in a recent event, typically associated with an earnings release or major company announcement, you can find the details in the most recent 8-K. Also, you may want to occasionally peruse the Form 4's to see if insiders have been trading company stock. Every time company insiders make a transaction in company stock, they are required to file the Form 4, allowing you a peek into whether they are buying or selling shares. While an insider's trading activity may be no smarter than your own, it can at least reveal if management's investment behavior is consistent with its tone.

Filing "Decoder Ring"

There are literally hundreds of different types of SEC filings. Below is your "decoder ring" for finding the most important ones.

10-K	Comprehensive annual report of a company. Contains audited financial statements.
10-Q	Quarterly report of a company. Contains less information than the 10-K and unaudited financial statements.
DEF 14A	Proxy statement. Annual report on management, board of directors, and shareholder voting.
8-K	A current report on the material events and corporate changes not previously reported.
Form 4	Notice of insider stock transactions.
20-F	Annual report for foreign companies listed in the U.S. Think of this as the 10-K for foreign firms.
40-F	Annual report for Canadian companies listed in the U.S. Think of this as the 10-K for Canadian firms.
PREM 14A	Preliminary proxy statement related to a merger or acquisition.

Making the Most of a Company Web Site

Another source of information is the company itself. Just plug the name of the company you want to research into the search engine of your choice. You should find the company Web site near the top of your results.

The investor section of a company's Web site can offer a variety of information. Copies of the public filings are usually available in more flexible, downloadable formats—such as PDF, Microsoft Excel, or Microsoft Word. Also, you can sort through the firm's press releases and examine the latest investor presentations (typically in PDF or Microsoft PowerPoint formats).

For a Cleaner Format

Don't want to read public filings on the Web? Or want a cleaner document to print? Several other sources of public filings are available. Some are free and some charge a small fee:

Check out the company Web site. (Companies typically make PDF, Microsoft Excel, and Microsoft Word versions of public filings available for free.)

The 10K Wizard www.10kwizard.com charges a small annual fee to gain access to PDF, Excel, and Word versions of public filings.

Edgar Pro www.edgarpro.com charges a small annual fee to gain access to PDF, Excel, and Word versions of public filings.

It's definitely worth a visit to the company Web site. It doesn't take long, and reading the press releases will give you some of the most up-to-date information available. Also, it may be useful to see how a company does business on the Web.

Setting Up a Watch List

After you've researched your first batch of companies (read the public filings and visited company Web sites), it's time to set up a watch list. How do you do this? Fortunately, many Web sites offer portfolio and watch-list services. In fact, Morningstar (www.morningstar.com) offers these services for free:

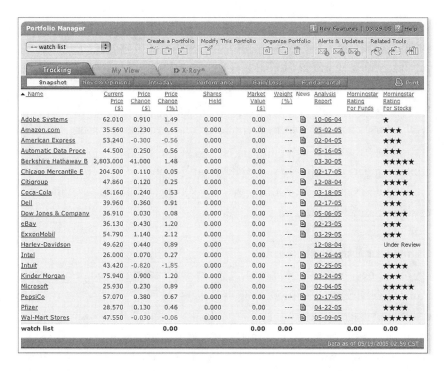

Portfolio Manager			New Features	08.29.05	Help

(toolbar: -- watch list | Create a Portfolio | Modify This Portfolio | Organize Portfolio | Alerts & Updates | Related Tools)

(tabs: Tracking | My View | X-Ray®)

(sub-tabs: Snapshot | News & Opinions | Intraday | Performance | Gain/Loss | Fundamental | Print)

▲ Name	Current Price ($)	Price Change ($)	Price Change (%)	Shares Held	Market Value ($)	Weight (%)	News	Analysis Report	Morningstar Rating For Funds	Morningstar Rating For Stocks
Adobe Systems	62.010	0.910	1.49	0.000	0.00	---	📄	10-06-04		★
Amazon.com	35.560	0.230	0.65	0.000	0.00	---	📄	05-02-05		★★★
American Express	53.240	-0.300	-0.56	0.000	0.00	---	📄	02-04-05		★★★
Automatic Data Proce	44.500	0.250	0.56	0.000	0.00	---	📄	05-16-05		★★★
Berkshire Hathaway B	2,803.000	41.000	1.48	0.000	0.00	---		03-30-05		★★★★★
Chicago Mercantile E	204.500	0.110	0.05	0.000	0.00	---	📄	02-17-05		★★★★
Citigroup	47.860	0.120	0.25	0.000	0.00	---	📄	12-08-04		★★★★
Coca-Cola	45.160	0.240	0.53	0.000	0.00	---	📄	03-18-05		★★★★★
Dell	39.960	0.360	0.91	0.000	0.00	---	📄	02-17-05		★★★
Dow Jones & Company	36.910	0.030	0.08	0.000	0.00	---	📄	05-06-05		★★★★
eBay	36.130	0.430	1.20	0.000	0.00	---	📄	02-23-05		★★★
ExxonMobil	54.790	1.140	2.12	0.000	0.00	---	📄	03-29-05		★★★
Harley-Davidson	49.620	0.440	0.89	0.000	0.00	---		12-08-04		Under Review
Intel	26.000	0.070	0.27	0.000	0.00	---	📄	04-26-05		★★★
Intuit	43.420	-0.820	-1.85	0.000	0.00	---	📄	02-25-05		★★★★
Kinder Morgan	75.940	0.900	1.20	0.000	0.00	---	📄	03-24-05		★★★
Microsoft	25.930	0.230	0.89	0.000	0.00	---	📄	02-04-05		★★★★★
PepsiCo	57.070	0.380	0.67	0.000	0.00	---	📄	02-17-05		★★★★
Pfizer	28.570	0.130	0.46	0.000	0.00	---	📄	04-22-05		★★★★
Wal-Mart Stores	47.550	-0.030	-0.06	0.000	0.00	---	📄	05-09-05		★★★★★
watch list		0.00			0.00	0.00			0.00	0.00

Data as of 05/19/2005 02:59 CST

1. Go to the Morningstar Web site (www.morningstar.com) and click on the tab labeled "Portfolio."

2. In the Portfolio Manager window, under "Create a Portfolio," click "New Portfolio."

3. You'll see a box labeled "Step 1." It's automatically set up to build a watch list, so click "Continue."

4. Pick a name for your portfolio, or just call it "watch list." Then, plug in the ticker symbols of the companies you want to watch. Click "Done."

5. In the following window, you'll see a list of updates, alerts, and tips that Morningstar will send you daily for the companies in your watch list. Click "Done" again.

6. Now you have a watch list that you can visit anytime by clicking the portfolio tab on Morningstar.com.

By creating a watch list, you'll be able to keep tabs on company news and easily find stock price information. Among other things, you can set alerts to notify you when a stock price has met or exceeded a particular threshold. Thus, your watch list will eventually become an integral tool in helping you make buy and sell decisions, stay organized, and keep informed.

Staying in Tune with Industry Web Sites

After you've uncovered some basic information about the companies on your watch list, you may hunger to learn even more. Industry-oriented Web sites are one way to deepen your knowledge and gain new insights. Nearly every industry has Web sites dedicated to publishing news, commentary, and general information that can help enhance your understanding of particular business environments. Some of the best types of Web sites include federal and local regulators, industry and trade organizations, and professional sites. We've included some of the Morningstar stock analyst team's favorite industry Web sites as an addendum on page 162.

Seeking Out Expert Opinions

After you've become a bit of an expert yourself by sifting through the information we've already discussed, you may want to read what other analysts and investors have to say about a particular company. While your investing decisions are yours to make, you might be able to gain a new insight or angle by reading others' research. Obviously, we think a subscription to Morningstar.com's Premium Membership service, which would allow you to read our analysts' opinions, is one worthwhile resource.

In addition, you may want to regularly read financial news available in Web and print publications. This may include financial newspapers like the *Wall Street Journal* or the *Financial Times*. You may find magazines like *Forbes*, *Fortune*, or *BusinessWeek* helpful sources of business-focused news as well. If you're interested in reading what other famous investors or fund managers have to say, you can visit fund company Web sites to read their quarterly commentaries.

Avoiding Information Overload

You shouldn't feel bad if you can't read every article from every source that comments on a company you're researching. In your journey to becoming an informed stock investor, you'll almost inevitably feel overwhelmed from time to time by the vast amounts of information available. Fortunately, you don't need to read it all to be successful. In fact, some information may actually harm your performance by taking your focus away from what's truly important. That's why we've highlighted the key pieces of information you will need to make an informed decision.

Here's a quick step-by-step guide to becoming informed about a company:

1. Obtain the firm's 10-K and really try to give it a thoughtful read. Don't feel bad if you spend a lot of time on this step. (Give it a couple of days to digest.)
2. Read through the 10-Qs when they are released each quarter. These are usually much shorter than the 10-K and shouldn't require more than an hour or two of your time.
3. Set up a watch list to organize the steady flow of news on all the companies that interest you.
4. Poke around on the company's Web site. This takes less than half an hour.
5. When time allows, visit relevant industry Web sites and catch up on some of the industry trends.

The Bottom Line

If you follow these steps, you'll be able to form a foundation of understanding about a company in about a week. Over time, you can build on your foundation and gain a much deeper understanding. Further, you'll be able to weed out the news that just isn't worth your time. All told, if you stay the course, you could be surprised how your knowledge will grow by applying this simple process.

Investor's Checklist

▸ When you begin researching a company, start by reading the 10-K. Published annually, the 10-K is a comprehensive report filled with information about a company, including its financial statements.

▸ Throughout the year, keep tabs on your company by reading the 10-Qs. Published quarterly, the 10-Q is smaller than the 10-K, but provides a more up-to-date report on your company.

▸ If you want to check up on executive compensation and recent shareholder votes, be sure to read the annual proxy statement, also known as form DEF 14A.

▸ Public filings like the 10-K, 10-Q, and proxy are posted on the SEC Web site www.sec.gov. You can read them free of charge.

▸ Be sure to visit a company's Web site. Often, it will post public filings in convenient electronic formats like PDF, Excel, and Word. Further, you'll be able to see how the company conducts business on the Web and view recent investor presentations.

▸ Don't let yourself get bogged down with too much information. However, if time allows and you're interested, visit industry Web sites to get a lay of the land.

Quiz

1 What is the must-read public filing that provides a comprehensive overview of a company and is published annually?

a	10-Q.
b	Form 4.
c	10-K.

Answers to this quiz can be found on page 168

2 Which public filing provides investors with a quarterly update?

a	10-Q.
b	Form 4.
c	10-K.

3 If you want to find out if the CEO is selling his or her stock or buying more, you should search which public filings?

a	10-Q.
b	Form 4.
c	10-K.

4 Which one of the following sources contains financial information audited by an independent accounting firm?

a	10-Q.
b	10-K.
c	Press release.

5 Which of the following sources is written from a point of view other than the company itself?

a	Press release.
b	10-Q.
c	Analyst research report.

Worksheet

Answers to this worksheet can be found on page 178

1 Procure a 10-K for a company you are interested in and give it a thorough read. Did it change the way you thought about the company? What risks or opportunities are you aware of now that you weren't before?

2 How do you plan to keep tabs on companies that interest you throughout the year? Have you built a watch list and read some of the public filings?

3 When you read your last proxy statement, did it seem like management was on your side? Were they paying themselves huge salaries despite poor company performance? Or did they have a meaningful stake in company stock? What parts of the proxy did you find most useful?

4 Consider the sources of the information you've used to better understand companies. How much of the information comes from the companies themselves? How can you gain different perspectives?

Lesson 107: Introduction to Financial Statements

"There's no business like show business, but there are several businesses like accounting."
—David Letterman

Although the words "financial statements" and "accounting" send cold shivers down many people's backs, this is the language of business, a language investors need to know before buying stocks. The beauty is you don't need to be a CPA to understand the basics of the three most fundamental and important financial statements: the income statement, the balance sheet, and the statement of cash flows. All three of these statements are found in a firm's annual report, 10-K, and 10-Q filings.

The financial statements are windows into a company's performance and health. We'll provide a very basic overview of each financial statement in this lesson, including examples from Harley-Davidson's 2004 annual report, and go into much greater detail in Workbook #2.

The Income Statement

What is it and why do I care?

The income statement tells you how much money a company has brought in (its revenues), how much it has spent (its expenses), and the difference between the two (its profit). The income statement shows a company's revenues and expenses over a specific time frame such as three months or a year. This statement contains the information you'll most often see mentioned in the press or in financial reports—figures such as total revenue, net income, or earnings per share.

Investors should be more concerned about a company's earnings per share, affectionately known as EPS, than about raw earnings. EPS shows how much profit the firm earned for each share of its stock outstanding. Therefore, if a company doubles its earnings in one year, but it also issues enough new shares that its total share count doubles, EPS would not change, and investors would be no better off.	**Earnings by Any Other Name**

Consolidated Statements of Income

(in thousands, except per-share amounts)

Years ended December 31,	2004	2003	2002
Net revenue	$ 5,015,190	$ 4,624,274	$ 4,090,970
Cost of goods sold	3,115,655	2,958,708	2,673,129
Gross profit	1,899,535	1,665,566	1,417,841
Financial services income	305,262	279,459	211,500
Financial services expense	116,662	111,586	107,273
Operating income from financial services	188,600	167,873	104,227
Selling, administrative and engineering expense	726,644	684,175	639,366
Income from operations	1,361,491	1,149,264	882,702
Investment income, net	23,101	23,088	16,541
Other, net	(5,106)	(6,317)	(13,416)
Income before provision for income taxes	1,379,486	1,166,035	885,827
Provision for income taxes	489,720	405,107	305,610
Net income	$ 889,766	$ 760,928	$ 580,217
Basic earnings per common share	$3.02	$2.52	$1.92
Diluted earnings per common share	$3.00	$2.50	$1.90
Cash dividends per common share	$.405	$.195	$.135

The accompanying notes are an integral part of the consolidated financial statements.

Example of income statement from Harley-Davidson.

The income statement answers the question, "How well is the company's business performing?" Or in simpler terms, "Is it making money?" A firm must be able to bring in more money than it spends or it won't be in business for very long. Firms with low expenses relative to revenues—and thus, high profits relative to revenues—are particularly desirable for investment because a bigger piece of each dollar the company brings in directly benefits you as a shareholder.

Revenues, Expenses, and Profits

Each of the three main elements of the income statement is described below.

Revenues. The revenue section is typically the simplest part of the income statement. Often, there is just a single number that represents all the money a company brought in during a specific time period, although big companies sometimes break down revenues in ways that provide more information (e.g., segregated by geographic location or business segment). Revenues are also commonly known as sales.

Expenses. Although there are many types of expenses, the two most common are the cost of sales and SG&A (selling, general, and administrative) expenses.

Cost of sales, which is also called cost of goods sold, is the expense most directly involved in creating revenue. For example, Gap may pay $10 to make a shirt, which it sells for $15. When it is sold, the cost of sales for that shirt would be $10—what it cost Gap to produce the shirt for sale.

Selling, general, and administrative expenses are also commonly known as operating expenses. This category includes most other costs in running a business, including marketing, management salaries, and technology expenses.

Profits. In its simplest form, profit is equal to total revenues minus total expenses. However, there are several commonly used profit subcategories investors should be aware of.

Gross profit is calculated as revenues minus cost of sales. It basically shows how much money is left over to pay for operating expenses (and hopefully provide profit to stockholders) after a sale is made. Using our example of the Gap shirt before, the gross profit from the sale of the shirt would have been $5 ($15 sales price - $10 cost of sales = $5 gross profit).

Operating profit is equal to revenues minus the cost of sales and SG&A. This number represents the profit a company made from its actual operations, and excludes certain expenses and revenues that may not be related to its central operations.

Net income generally represents the company's profit after all expenses, including financial expenses, have been paid. This number is often called the "bottom line" and is generally the figure people refer to when they use the word "profit" or "earnings."

The Balance Sheet

What is it and why do I care?

The balance sheet, also known as the statement of financial condition, basically tells you how much a company owns (its assets), and how much it owes (its liabilities). The difference between what it owns and what it owes is its equity, also commonly called "net assets," "stockholder's equity," or "net worth."

For Equation Lovers	On the balance sheet, assets will always equal the sum of liabilities and equity. This is often called the basic accounting equation.
	Equity ⊕ Liabilities ⊖ Assets **or** Assets ⊖ Liabilities ⊖ Equity

The balance sheet provides investors with a snapshot of a company's health as of the date provided on the financial statement. Generally, if a company

70

has lots of assets relative to liabilities, it's in good shape. Conversely, just as you would be cautious loaning money to a friend who is burdened with large debts, a company with a large amount of liabilities relative to assets should be scrutinized more carefully.

Consolidated Balance Sheets

(in thousands, except share amounts)

December 31,	2004	2003
ASSETS		
Current assets:		
Cash and cash equivalents	$ 275,159	$ 329,329
Marketable securities	1,336,909	993,331
Accounts receivable, net	121,333	112,406
Current portion of finance receivables, net	1,207,124	1,001,990
Inventories	226,893	207,726
Deferred income taxes	60,517	51,156
Prepaid expenses and other current assets	38,337	33,189
Total current assets	3,266,272	2,729,127
Finance receivables, net	905,176	735,859
Property, plant and equipment, net	1,024,665	1,046,310
Goodwill	59,456	53,678
Other assets	227,724	358,114
	$ 5,483,293	$4,923,088
LIABILITIES AND SHAREHOLDERS' EQUITY		
Current liabilities:		
Accounts payable	$ 244,202	$ 223,902
Accrued expenses and other liabilities	433,053	407,566
Current portion of finance debt	495,441	324,305
Total current liabilities	1,172,696	955,773
Finance debt	800,000	670,000
Other long-term liabilities	90,846	86,337
Postretirement healthcare benefits	149,848	127,444
Deferred income taxes	51,432	125,842
Commitments and contingencies (Note 6)		
Shareholders' equity:		
Series A Junior participating preferred stock, none issued	—	—
Common stock, 329,908,165 and 326,489,291 shares issued in 2004 and 2003, respectively	3,300	3,266
Additional paid-in capital	533,068	419,455
Retained earnings	3,844,571	3,074,037
Accumulated other comprehensive (loss) income	(12,096)	47,174
	4,368,843	3,543,932
Less:		
Treasury stock (35,597,360 and 24,978,798 shares in 2004 and 2003, respectively), at cost	(1,150,372)	(586,240)
Total shareholders' equity	3,218,471	2,957,692
	$ 5,483,293	$4,923,088

The accompanying notes are an integral part of the consolidated financial statements.

52

Example of balance sheet from Harley-Davidson.

Assets, Liabilities, and Equity

Each of the three primary elements of the balance sheet is described below.

Assets. There are two main types of assets: current assets and noncurrent assets. Within these two categories, there are numerous subcategories, many of which will be explained in Workbook #2.

Current assets are likely to be used up or converted into cash within one business cycle—usually defined as one year. For example, the groceries at your local supermarket would be classified as current assets because apples and bananas should be sold within the next year.

Noncurrent assets are defined by our left-brained accountant friends as, you guessed it, anything not classified as a current asset. For example, the refrigerators at your supermarket would be classified as noncurrent assets because it's unlikely they will be "used up" or converted to cash within a year.

Fancy Name, but the Same Balance Sheet	The balance sheet is often referred to as the statement of financial condition.

Liabilities. Similar to assets, there are two main categories of liabilities: current liabilities and noncurrent liabilities.

Current liabilities are obligations the firm must pay within a year. For example, your supermarket may have bought and received $1,000 worth of eggs from a local farm but won't pay for them until next month.

Noncurrent liabilities are the flip side of noncurrent assets. These liabilities represent money the company owes one year or more in the future. For example, the grocer may borrow $1 million from a bank for a new store, which it must pay back in five years.

Equity. Equity represents the part of the company that is owned by shareholders; thus, it's commonly referred to as shareholder's equity. As described above, equity is equal to total assets minus total liabilities. Although there are several categories within equity, the two biggest are paid-in capital and retained earnings.

Paid-in capital is the amount of money shareholders paid for their shares when the stock was first offered to the public. It basically represents how much money the firm received when it sold its shares.

Retained earnings represent the total profits the company has earned since it began, minus whatever has been paid to shareholders as dividends. Since this is a cumulative number, if a company has lost money over time, retained earnings can be negative and would be renamed "accumulated deficit."

The Statement of Cash Flows

What is it and why do I care?

The statement of cash flows tells you how much cash went into and out of a company during a specific time frame such as a quarter or a year. You may wonder why there's a need for such a statement because it sounds very similar to the income statement, which shows how much revenue came in and how many expenses went out.

Accrual Accounting in Action

Assume that Dawn's Bouquets sold $1,000 worth of flowers on Sept. 29 to Wayne, but he couldn't pay until October. If you looked at Dawn's Bouquets' income statement for the three-month period ending on Sept. 30, you'd see that the $1,000 was recorded as revenue even though it wasn't received yet. However, the statement of cash flows for the same time period wouldn't count the transaction because the cash had not been collected.

The difference lies in a complex concept called accrual accounting. Accrual accounting requires companies to record revenues and expenses when transactions occur, not when cash is exchanged. While that explanation seems simple enough, it's a big mess in practice, and the statement of cash flows helps investors sort it out.

CONSOLIDATED STATEMENTS

Consolidated Statements of Cash Flows

(in thousands)

Years ended December 31,	2004	2003	2002
Cash flows from operating activities:			
Net income	$ 889,766	$ 760,928	$ 580,217
Adjustments to reconcile net income to net cash provided by operating activities:			
Depreciation	214,112	196,918	175,778
Provision for long-term employee benefits	62,806	76,422	57,124
Provision for finance credit losses	3,070	4,076	6,167
Gain on current year securitizations	(58,302)	(82,221)	(56,139)
Net change in wholesale finance receivables	(154,124)	(154,788)	(140,107)
Contributions to pension plans	—	(192,000)	(153,636)
Tax benefit from the exercise of stock options	51,476	13,805	14,452
Deferred income taxes	(41,513)	42,105	38,560
Other	27,301	16,051	7,057
Net changes in current assets and current liabilities	(24,866)	(18,644)	16,089
Total adjustments	79,960	(98,276)	(34,655)
Net cash provided by operating activities	969,726	662,652	545,562
Cash flows from investing activities:			
Capital expenditures	(213,550)	(227,230)	(323,866)
Finance receivables acquired or originated	(2,394,644)	(2,090,201)	(1,731,169)
Finance receivables collected	274,670	252,705	230,153
Proceeds from securitizations	1,847,895	1,724,060	1,246,262
Collection of retained securitization interests	135,732	118,113	89,970
Purchase of marketable securities	(1,091,326)	(1,538,548)	(1,508,285)
Sales and redemptions of marketable securities	742,284	1,145,000	1,253,719
Purchase of remaining interest in joint venture	(9,500)	—	—
Other, net	10,680	9,690	22,813
Net cash used in investing activities	(707,750)	(606,411)	(720,403)
Cash flows from financing activities:			
Proceeds from issuance of medium-term notes	—	399,953	—
Net increase (decrease) finance credit facilities and commercial paper	305,047	(175,835)	165,528
Dividends paid	(119,232)	(58,986)	(41,457)
Purchase of common stock for treasury	(564,132)	(103,880)	(56,814)
Issuance of common stock under employee stock option plans	62,171	19,378	12,679
Net cash (used) provided by financing activities	(316,146)	80,630	79,936
Net increase (decrease) in cash and cash equivalents	(54,170)	136,871	(94,905)
Cash and cash equivalents:			
At beginning of year	329,329	192,458	287,363
At end of year	$ 275,159	$ 329,329	$ 192,458

The accompanying notes are an integral part of the consolidated financial statements.

Example of statement of cash flows from Harley-Davidson.

The statement of cash flows is very important to investors because it shows how much actual cash a company has generated. The income statement, on the other hand, often includes noncash revenues or expenses, which the statement of cash flows excludes.

One of the most important traits you should seek in a potential investment is the firm's ability to generate cash. Many companies have shown profits on the income statement but stumbled later because of insufficient cash flows. A good look at the statement of cash flows for those companies may have warned investors that rocky times were ahead.

The Three Elements of the Statement of Cash Flows

Because companies can generate and use cash in several different ways, the statement of cash flows is separated into three sections: cash flows from operating activities, from investing activities, and from financing activities.

The cash flows from operating activities section shows how much cash the company generated from its core business, as opposed to peripheral activities such as investing or borrowing. Investors should look closely at how much cash a firm generates from its operating activities because it paints the best picture of how well the business is producing cash that will ultimately benefit shareholders.

Free cash flow is a term you will become very familiar with over the course of these workbooks. In simple terms, it represents the amount of excess cash a company generated, which can be used to enrich shareholders or invest in new opportunities for the business without hurting the existing operation; thus, it's considered "free." Although there are many methods of determining free cash flow, the most common method is taking the net cash flows provided by operating activities and subtracting capital expenditures (as found in the "cash flows from investing activities" section).

Cash from Operations ⊖ Capital Expenditures ⊖ Free Cash Flow

Shareholders Get Something for "Free"

The cash flows from investing activities section shows the amount of cash firms spent on investments. Investments are usually classified as either capital expenditures—money spent on items such as new equipment or anything else needed to keep the business running—or monetary investments such as the purchase or sale of money market funds.

The cash flows from financing activities section includes any activities involved in transactions with the company's owners or debtors. For example, cash proceeds from new debt, or dividends paid to investors would be found in this section.

The Bottom Line

Phew!!! You made it through an entire lesson about financial statements. While we're the first to acknowledge that there are far more exciting aspects about investing in stocks than learning about accounting and financial statements, it's essential for investors to know the language of business. We also recommend you sharpen your newfound language skills by taking a good look at the more-detailed discussion on financial statements in Workbook #2.

Investor's Checklist

► Financial statements provide investors with a look into the financial health and performance of companies. The income statement, balance sheet, and statement of cash flows—which are found in every financial filing for all public companies—are the most important financial statements for investors to understand.

► The income statement shows how much profit a company has made for its shareholders over a specific time period such as a quarter or a year. A firm's profit is equal to how much it has brought in (revenues) minus how much it has spent (expenses).

► The balance sheet provides a snapshot of how much a company owns (assets) and how much it owes (liabilities) at a specific point in time. The difference between what a firm owns and what it owes is known as equity, the amount of the company owned by shareholders.

► The statement of cash flows shows how much cash has flowed into and out of a company over a specific time period. This statement separates a company's cash flows among three categories: cash flows from operating activities, cash flows from investing activities, and cash flows from financing activities.

► Free cash flow—which represents excess cash generated by a company that can either be paid to investors or used for new opportunities for the business—is determined from the statement of cash flows by taking net cash provided from operating activities and subtracting capital expenditures (from the "cash flows from investing activities" section).

Quiz

Answers to this quiz can be found on page 168

1   On the income statement, profits tell you:

a	The difference between how much a company owns and how much it owes.
b	The difference between how much a company brought in and how much it spent during a given period.
c	The difference between how much a company owns and how much it spent during a given period.

2   Which of the following is *not* a part of the statement of cash flows?

a	Cash flows from operating activities.
b	Cash flows from financing activities.
c	Cash flows from expense activities.

3   A company with lots of assets relative to liabilities on its balance sheet:

a	Is in danger of going bankrupt.
b	Has very little equity.
c	Is healthier than a company with lots of liabilities.

4   Current assets are:

a	Assets likely to be used up or converted into cash within the next year.
b	Assets likely to be used up or converted into cash within the next three years.
c	Assets a company does not own yet.

5   What is a major difference between the income statement and the statement of cash flows?

a	The statement of cash flows refers to a single point in time, rather than a period of time like a quarter or a year.
b	The statement of cash flows excludes noncash revenues and expenses.
c	The statement of cash flows provides a breakdown of revenues, expenses, and profits.

Worksheet

1   What are the main things an investor will learn from looking at the income statement? Balance sheet? Statement of cash flows?

Answers to this worksheet can be found on page 179

2   Your most recent stock investment, Mark's Music, just reported some of its year-end numbers. The firm showed total assets of $110 million and total equity of $60 million. How much are the firm's total liabilities?

3   What is the difference between these three measures of profit as found on the income statement: gross profit, operating profit, and net income?

4   In your own words, explain why a statement of cash flows is needed.

Lesson 108: Learn the Lingo—Basic Ratios

"I understand a fury in your words, But not the words."—William Shakespeare

Now that you've learned the basics of reading financial statements (the language of business), let's learn the basic language of investing.

Ratios are a common tool investors use to relate a stock's price with an element of the underlying company's performance. These quick and dirty ratios can be useful in their own way, as long as you're aware of the limitations.

But before we get to calculating any ratios, we must first cover some essential definitions.

Earnings Per Share

Earnings per share (EPS) is a company's net income (typically over the trailing 12 months) divided by its number of shares outstanding. EPS comes in two varieties, basic and diluted. Basic EPS includes only actual outstanding shares of a company's stock, while diluted EPS represents all potential stock that could be outstanding with current stock option grants and the like. Diluted EPS is the more "conservative" number.

$$\text{EPS} = \frac{\text{Total Company Earnings}}{\text{Shares Outstanding}}$$

Although EPS can give you a quick idea of a company's profitability, it should not be used in isolation without also looking at cash flow and other performance metrics.

Market Capitalization

Market capitalization is essentially the market value of a company. It is calculated by multiplying the number of shares outstanding by the current share price. For example, if there are 10 million shares outstanding of ABC Corporation and ABC's stock is currently trading at $25 per share, the market capitalization of ABC is $250 million. As we will find out shortly, market capitalization not only gives you an idea concerning the size of a company, it can also be used when calculating the basic valuation ratios.

$$\text{Market Capitalization} = \text{Stock Price} \times \text{Shares Outstanding}$$

Profit Margins

Just as there are three types of profits—gross, operating, and net—there are also three types of profit margins that can be calculated to offer insight into a company's profitability. Gross margin is simply gross profits divided by revenues, and so on. Margins are usually stated in percentages.

$$\text{Gross Margin} = \frac{\text{Gross Profits}}{\text{Revenues}} \qquad \text{Operating Margin} = \frac{\text{Operating Profits}}{\text{Revenues}}$$

$$\text{Net Margin} = \frac{\text{Net Profits}}{\text{Revenues}}$$

Price/Earnings and Related Ratios

One of the most popular valuation measures is the price/earnings ratio, or P/E. The P/E is the price of a stock divided by its EPS from the trailing four quarters. As an example, a stock trading for $15 per share with earnings of $1 per share during the past year has a P/E of 15.

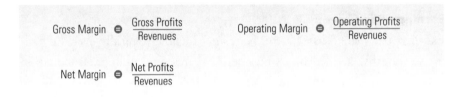

$$\text{P/E} = \frac{\text{Stock Price}}{\text{EPS}} = \frac{\text{Market Capitalization}}{\text{Total Company Profits}}$$

The P/E ratio gives a rough idea of the price investors are paying for a stock relative to its underlying earnings. It is a quick and dirty way to gauge how cheap or expensive a stock may be. Generally, the higher the P/E ratio, the more investors are willing to pay for a dollar's worth of earnings from a company. High P/E stocks (typically those with a P/E above 30) tend to have higher growth rates and/or the expectation of a profit turnaround. Meanwhile, low P/E stocks (typically those with a P/E below 15) tend to have slower growth and/or lesser future prospects.

The P/E ratio can also be useful when compared with the P/Es of similar companies to see how the competitors stack up. In addition, you can compare a company's P/E with the average P/E of the S&P 500 or some other benchmark index to get a rough idea of how richly a stock is valued relative to the broader market.

The "E" part of EPS and P/E can be tricky. Sometimes a company can incur one-time expenses that temporarily take a big bite out of earnings and jack up the P/E. Also, make sure you're using comparable "Es." Forward P/E is another very common ratio that calculates P/E using a consensus of Wall Street's projected earnings for the current fiscal year. A company's forward P/E will be lower than a trailing P/E if a company's earnings are growing from year to year.

Watch the "E" in P/E

One useful variant of P/E is earnings yield, or EPS divided by the stock price. Earnings yield is the inverse of P/E, so a high earnings yield indicates a relatively inexpensive stock while a low earnings yield indicates a more expensive one. It can be useful to compare earnings yields with 10- or 30-year Treasury bond yields to get an idea of how expensive a stock is.

$$\text{Earnings Yield} = \frac{1}{\text{P/E Ratio}} = \frac{\text{EPS}}{\text{Stock Price}}$$

Another useful variant of P/E is the PEG ratio. A high P/E generally means that the market expects the company to grow its profits rapidly in the future, so a much greater percentage of the company's potential earnings are in the future. This means its market value (which reflects those future earnings) is large relative to its present-day earnings.

The PEG ratio can help you determine if a stock's P/E has gotten too high in these cases by giving you an idea of how much investors are paying for a company's growth. A stock's PEG ratio is its forward P/E divided by its expected earnings growth over the next five years as predicted by a consensus of Wall Street estimates. For example, if a company has a forward P/E of 20 with annual earnings estimated to grow 10% per year on average, its PEG ratio is 2.0. Again, the higher the PEG ratio, the more relatively expensive a stock is.

$$\text{PEG} = \frac{\text{Forward P/E Ratio}}{\text{5-Year EPS Growth Rate}}$$

Warning on PEG

As with other measures, the PEG ratio should be used with caution. PEG relies on two different Wall Street analyst estimates—next year's earnings and five-year earnings growth—and thus is doubly subject to the possibility of overly optimistic or pessimistic analysts. It also breaks down at the extremes of zero-growth or hyper-growth companies.

Price/Sales Ratio

The price/sales (P/S) ratio is figured the same way as P/E, except with a company's annual sales as the denominator instead of its earnings. An advantage to using the P/S ratio is that it is based on sales, a figure that is much harder to manipulate and is subject to fewer accounting estimates than earnings. Also, because sales tend to be more stable than earnings, P/S can be a good tool for screening cyclical companies and other companies with fluctuating earnings patterns.

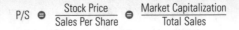

$$\text{P/S} = \frac{\text{Stock Price}}{\text{Sales Per Share}} = \frac{\text{Market Capitalization}}{\text{Total Sales}}$$

When using the P/S ratio, it is important to keep in mind that a dollar of earnings has essentially the same value regardless of the level of sales needed to create it. Meaning, a dollar of sales at a highly profitable firm is worth more than a dollar of sales for a company with narrow profit margins. This means comparing price/sales is generally useful only when comparing companies in similar industries.

To understand the differences across industries, let's compare grocery stores with the medical-device industry. Grocery stores tend to have very small profit margins, earning only a few pennies on each dollar of sales. As such, grocers have an average P/S ratio of 0.5, one of the lowest in Morningstar's coverage universe. It takes a lot of sales to create a dollar of earnings at a grocery store, so investors do not value those sales dollars very highly.

Meanwhile, medical-device makers have much fatter profit margins. Relative to the grocer, it does not take nearly as much in sales for a medical-device company to create a dollar in earnings. It is little wonder the device makers have a high average price/sales ratio of 5.0. A grocer with a P/S ratio of 2.0 would look quite expensive while a medical-device maker with the same P/S could be dirt-cheap.

Price/Book Ratio

Another common valuation measure is the price/book ratio (P/B), which relates a stock's market value with its book value (also known as shareholder equity) from the latest balance sheet. Book value can be thought of as what would be left over for shareholders if a company shutters operations, pays off its creditors, collects from its debtors, and liquidates itself.

$$\text{Book Value Per Share} = \frac{\text{Total Shareholder Equity}}{\text{Shares Outstanding}}$$

$$\text{P/B} = \frac{\text{Stock Price}}{\text{Book Value Per Share}} = \frac{\text{Market Capitalization}}{\text{Total Shareholder Equity}}$$

As with the other ratios we've covered so far, there are caveats to using P/B. For instance, book value may not accurately measure a company's worth, especially if the firm possesses significant intangible assets such as brand names, market share, and other competitive advantages. The lowest price/book ratios tend to be in capital-intensive industries such as utilities and retail, whereas the highest P/B ratios are in fields such as pharmaceuticals and consumer products, where intangibles are more important.

Price/book is also tied to return on equity (ROE), which is net income divided by shareholder equity. (We will talk more about ROE in Workbook #2.) Given two companies that are otherwise equal, the one with the higher ROE will have a higher P/B ratio. A high P/B shouldn't be cause for alarm, especially if the company continually earns a high ROE.

Price/Cash Flow

The price/cash flow (P/CF) ratio is not as commonly used or as well known as the other measures we've discussed. It's calculated similarly to P/E, except that it uses operating cash flow instead of net income as the denominator.

$$P/CF = \frac{\text{Stock Price}}{\text{Operating Cash Flow Per Share}} = \frac{\text{Market Capitalization}}{\text{Total Operating Cash Flow}}$$

Cash flow can be less subject to accounting shenanigans than earnings because it measures actual cash, not paper or accounting profits. Price/cash flow can be helpful for firms such as utilities and cable companies, which can have more cash flow than reported earnings. Price/cash flow can also be used in place of P/E when there are so many one-time expenses that reported earnings are negative.

Dividend Yield

There are two ways to make money when buying a stock—capital gains (when a stock goes up in price) and dividend payments. Dividends are payments that companies make directly to shareholders.

Dividend yield has been an important measure of valuation for many years. The dividend yield is equal to a company's annual dividend per share divided by its stock price per share. So, if a company pays an annual dividend of $2.00 and has a stock that trades for $100, its dividend yield is 2.0%. If that same stock's price fell to $50 per share, its dividend yield would rise to 4.0%. Conversely, all else equal, the dividend yield falls when a stock's price goes up.

$$\text{Dividend Yield} = \frac{\text{Annual Dividends Per Share}}{\text{Stock Price}}$$

Stocks with high dividend yields are generally mature companies with few growth opportunities. The economic reasoning behind this is that these companies can't find enough promising projects to invest in for future growth, so they pay a larger portion of profits back to shareholders. While utility companies are considered the typical dividend-paying stocks, you can also find dividends in sectors with lots of room left for growth such as the pharmaceutical industry.

Dividends have recently begun to garner investors' attention again. A big driver of this new focus was a recent change in the United States tax code that lowered the tax rate on dividends. (Read ahead to the next lesson for more on this.) So if you are looking for dividend income from your stock investments, remember that the best high-yielding stocks have strong cash flows, healthy balance sheets, and relatively stable businesses. And, if you're relying on that stream of dividends for income, checking for a steady history of dividend payments is also a good idea.

Dividend Safety

Many investors may be attracted to stocks with high dividend yields. But it is important to remember that dividends are only as safe as the companies that pay them. Dividends are not guaranteed and can be cut by a company on a moment's notice. Healthy firms rarely cut their dividends, while cutting is a common practice among companies that are on the ropes.

The Bottom Line

We've gone over how to calculate a lot of ratios in this lesson, but understanding the components of these ratios is key to learning the lingo of investors. It is also essential in beginning to understand when a stock is cheap or expensive. The good news is that if you invest long enough, the ratios highlighted here will become second nature.

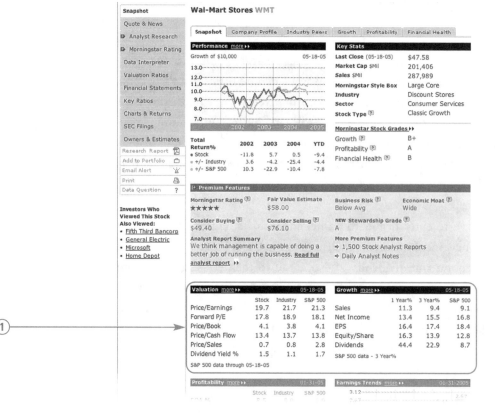

Example of where to find many of the terms defined in this lesson.

Investor's Checklist

▶ Valuation ratios are a quick and dirty way to evaluate a company's stock price. A recap of the most commonly used figures and ratios is below.

$$\text{EPS} = \frac{\text{Total Company Earnings}}{\text{Shares Outstanding}}$$

$$\text{Market Capitalization} = \text{Stock Price} \times \text{Shares Outstanding}$$

$$\text{Gross Margin} = \frac{\text{Gross Profits}}{\text{Revenues}}$$

$$\text{Net Margin} = \frac{\text{Net Profits}}{\text{Revenues}}$$

$$\text{Operating Margin} = \frac{\text{Operating Profits}}{\text{Revenues}}$$

$$\text{P/E} = \frac{\text{Stock Price}}{\text{EPS}} = \frac{\text{Market Capitalization}}{\text{Total Company Profits}}$$

$$\text{Earnings Yield} = \frac{1}{\text{P/E Ratio}} = \frac{\text{EPS}}{\text{Stock Price}}$$

$$\text{PEG} = \frac{\text{Forward P/E Ratio}}{\text{5-Year EPS Growth Rate}}$$

$$\text{P/S} = \frac{\text{Stock Price}}{\text{Sales Per Share}} = \frac{\text{Market Capitalization}}{\text{Total Sales}}$$

$$\text{Book Value Per Share} = \frac{\text{Total Shareholder Equity}}{\text{Shares Outstanding}}$$

$$\text{P/B} = \frac{\text{Stock Price}}{\text{Book Value Per Share}} = \frac{\text{Market Capitalization}}{\text{Total Shareholder Equity}}$$

$$\text{P/CF} = \frac{\text{Stock Price}}{\text{Operating Cash Flow Per Share}} = \frac{\text{Market Capitalization}}{\text{Total Operating Cash Flow}}$$

$$\text{Dividend Yield} = \frac{\text{Annual Dividends Per Share}}{\text{Stock Price}}$$

Quiz

Answers to this quiz can be found on page 169

1   If a company has earned $1.50 per share and its share price is $30, what is its P/E?

a	30.
b	5.
c	20.

2   If a company's P/E is 30, its earnings yield is:

a	3.0%.
b	3.3%.
c	30 times the company's earnings.

3   If two companies both have the same level of revenue, but company A turns more of every sales dollar into profit than company B, which will probably have a higher price/sales ratio?

a	Company A.
b	Company B.
c	Doesn't matter.

4   All else equal, what does a rising dividend yield mean for a stock?

a	The stock is becoming less expensive.
b	The stock is becoming more expensive.
c	It has no relation to how expensive a stock is.

5   What measure could you use for a company with negative earnings?

a	P/S.
b	P/CF.
c	Both.

Worksheet

1   What are some quick and dirty ways to check how expensive a stock is?

Answers to this worksheet can be found on page 179

2   Why is P/CF sometimes a more useful measure than P/E?

3   Assume we have a company with these characteristics:

Shares Outstanding = 10 million   Total Earnings = $25 million
Market Capitalization = $500 million

Calculate the following:

Stock Price?   P/E?

EPS?   Earnings Yield?

4   Assume we have a company with these characteristics:

Shareholder Equity = $10 billion   Shares Outstanding = 1 billion
Stock Price = $20   Annual Divided Per Share = $1.00

Calculate the following:

Market Capitalization?   P/B?

Book Value Per Share?   Dividend Yield?

Nuts and Bolts of
Stock Investing

Lesson 109: Stocks and Taxes

"But in this world nothing is certain but death and taxes."—*Benjamin Franklin*

Unlike death, taxation can at least be minimized. In this section, we will examine the basic framework of individual taxation in the United States as it relates to stock investing and review some simple steps you can take to be a more tax-efficient investor.

The information in this lesson is not necessarily exclusive to stock investing; much of it is also relevant to mutual fund investing. Nevertheless, if you are going to invest in any asset class, including stocks, it is imperative to understand exactly how taxes work so you may keep as many dollars as possible in your pocket and away from Uncle Sam.

Seek Advice

The Internal Revenue Code and accompanying regulations are incredibly complex. There are numerous exceptions to every rule, and exceptions to those exceptions. This lesson is intended to merely hit the highlights of investment taxation, and you should consult with a tax advisor to fully understand the range of tax consequences of your stock investing.

Ordinary Income Versus Capital Gains

Capital gains—the difference between what you sell a stock for versus what you paid for it—are "tax preferred," or taxed at lower rates than ordinary income. Ordinary income includes items such as wages and interest income. Capital gains arise when you sell a capital asset, such as a stock, for more than its purchase price, or basis. Conversely, you realize a capital loss when you sell the asset for less than its basis.

What Is a Capital Gain?

$6,000		
	Sold 100 shares of Acme at $50 per share ($5,000)	◄ Capital Gain: $1,000 ($10 per share)
$4,000	Bought 100 shares of Acme at $40 per share ($4,000)	
$2,000		

Capital gains are further subdivided into short term and long term. If a stock is sold within one year of purchase, the gain is short term and is taxed at the higher ordinary income rate. On the other hand, if you hold the stock for more than a year before selling, the gain is long term and is taxed at the lower capital gains rate.

Using Capital Losses

When you sell a stock for less than its basis, you realize a capital loss. While it is never fun to lose money, you can reduce your tax bill by using capital losses to offset capital gains. Also, to the extent that capital losses exceed capital gains, you can deduct the losses against your other income up to an annual limit of $3,000. Any additional loss above the $3,000 threshold is carried over to be used in subsequent years.

Jobs & Growth Tax Relief Reconciliation Act of 2003

Among other things, the 2003 tax cut (known affectionately as JGTRRA) lowered the tax rate for both long-term capital gains and qualified dividends to 15% for most taxpayers, and to 5% for taxpayers whose income places them in the 10% or 15% income tax brackets.

Since the basic idea behind the dividend tax cut was to reduce the burden of "double taxation," or taxation of the same profits at both the corporate and shareholder level, any dividends paid out of profits not subject to corporate taxation will not be considered "qualified dividends" eligible for the reduced tax rate. Therefore, one notable exception is dividends from real estate investment trusts, or REITs, which are typically still taxed at ordinary income rates. In addition, to qualify for the reduced dividend tax rate, you must have held a stock for at least 60 days out of the 120-day period beginning 60 days before the ex-dividend date (the date on which you must be holding a stock to receive the dividend).

If you want to take advantage of a capital loss, it is important that you keep the wash sale rule in mind. The rule states that you cannot claim a loss if you purchase substantially identical securities 30 days before or after the sale of the stock. For example, if on Dec. 30 you sell a stock for a loss but repurchase the same stock a few weeks later on Jan. 15, the wash sale rule prevents you from claiming the loss.

Beware the Wash Sale Rule

Unless the provisions of the 2003 tax cut are extended, the lower rates for long-term capital gains and qualified dividends will expire in 2009. In that year, the old 20% and 10% rates for capital gains will return, and all dividends will again be taxed at ordinary income rates. However, in 2008, the special 5% tax rate for lower-income taxpayers will drop to 0%.

Tax-Advantaged Accounts

One easy way to become a more tax-efficient stock investor is to utilize tax-advantaged accounts such as 401(k)s and individual retirement accounts (IRAs). These special accounts allow you to enjoy either tax-deferred or tax-free growth of your investments.

As you can see from the following graph, tax deferral can lead to significant savings over time. Let's assume two investors each start with $10,000 and earn a 10% annual return for 30 years. One has 100% of her gains tax-deferred, while the other realizes the full amount of his capital gains each year and pays a 20% tax on those gains. Under this scenario, the tax-deferred investor ends up with almost $75,000 more at the end than the investor with the taxable gains.

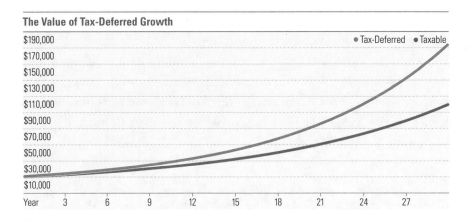

The Value of Tax-Deferred Growth

Clearly, it is worthwhile to learn about the types of tax-advantaged accounts available. Below are some of the most popular:

401(k)s

401(k) plans, so named after a section of the Internal Revenue Code, are set up by employers as a retirement-savings vehicle. The primary advantage of a 401(k) is tax deferral. First, employees can contribute a percentage of their income from each paycheck to their own 401(k) accounts on a pretax basis. This means the amount you contribute to your 401(k) is exempt from current federal income tax. For example, if you are in the 25% income tax bracket, a $100 contribution will reduce your current tax burden by $25. Second, dividends and capital gains earned inside a 401(k) are not subject to current taxation. In short, 401(k) plans allow you to defer taxation on dividends, capital gains, and a portion of your wages until you begin withdrawing from the plan, presumably during retirement, when you may be in a lower tax bracket. (All withdrawals are taxed at ordinary income rates.)

The amount you can contribute to your 401(k) plan is limited to $14,000 in 2005 and $15,000 in 2006. Thereafter, the annual contribution limit can be adjusted in $500 increments to account for inflation. You also must begin mandatory withdrawals from your 401(k) when you reach age 70 1/2. Withdrawals made before you turn 59 1/2 are taxed as ordinary income, and you may be subject to an additional 10% penalty.

Traditional IRAs

Individual retirement accounts are another vehicle for tax deferral. When you contribute to a traditional IRA, the IRS allows you to take an income tax deduction up to the amount of the contribution, subject to income limitations. In addition, dividends and capital gains earned inside a traditional IRA are not subject to tax until withdrawal.

However, there are some important limitations to remember. First, you must be age 70 1/2 or under with earned income to contribute to a traditional IRA. Second, the annual contribution limit is $4,000 from 2005 to 2007. The limit rises to $5,000 in 2008, and thereafter can be adjusted in $500 increments to account for inflation. If you are age 50 or older, you can make additional "catch-up" contributions of $500 in 2005 and $1,000 from 2006 onward. Finally, like 401(k) plans, you must begin mandatory withdrawals when you reach age 70 1/2. Withdrawals made before you turn 59 1/2 are taxed and may be subject to an additional 10% penalty.

Roth IRAs

These are typically the best retirement account option for many taxpayers. As with traditional IRAs, interest income, dividends, and capital gains accumulate tax-free. However, the main feature of Roth IRAs is that they are funded with after-tax dollars (contributions are not tax deductible). The upside of this is that qualified distributions from a Roth IRA are exempt from federal taxation.

The Roth IRA has the same annual contribution limits and "catch-up" provisions as a traditional IRA, but you must meet certain income requirements to contribute to a Roth IRA. Generally, single filers with income up to $95,000 and joint filers with income up to $150,000 are eligible to make the full annual contribution to a Roth IRA. Contributions to a Roth IRA can be withdrawn at any time without paying taxes or penalties, but withdrawal of earnings may be subject to income taxation and a 10% early withdrawal penalty if made before you turn 59 1/2.

Qualified Roth IRA Distributions	To qualify for tax-free treatment, a Roth IRA distribution must be (1) made after you become age 59 1/2; or (2) made after you become disabled as defined by the Internal Revenue Code; or (3) made to your beneficiary or estate after you die; or (4) used for a qualified first-time home purchase. In addition, the distribution must also be after a five-tax-year period from the time a contribution or conversion is first made into any Roth IRA. For example, if you open your first Roth IRA and make your first contribution on April 15, 2005, for the 2004 tax year, your five-year period starts on Jan. 1, 2004. Assuming you meet the other requirements, distributions made in this case after Dec. 31, 2008, from any Roth IRA will receive tax-free treatment.

Tax Planning 101

Besides taking advantage of 401(k) and IRA accounts, you can also follow a few basic planning strategies for investments held in taxable accounts. However, you should keep in mind that your goal as an investor should be to achieve the highest after-tax rate of return, not to avoid paying taxes. Taxes are a consideration, but they should not control your investment decisions.

The Value of Deferral and Stepped-Up Basis

All things being equal, it is better to pay taxes later than sooner. Therefore, you should endeavor to defer taxation as long as possible. An investor who purchases the shares of sound businesses and patiently holds them will not only enjoy the benefits of tax-free compounding, but will also save on brokerage commissions. At the least, toward the end of the year, you should consider delaying the realization of capital gains until January to defer your tax liability until the following year.

If you are extremely patient and die still owning a stock, your beneficiaries will receive the stock with a "stepped-up" basis, or a basis equal to the market value on the date of your death. Your beneficiaries can then sell the stock and owe no tax on the capital gains accumulated during your lifetime. There are special limitations on basis step-up if you happen to die in 2010, but after that year, the rule returns in its current form.

Wait for Long-Term Capital Gain Treatment

If you purchased a stock on Jan. 1, 2005, selling it for a gain on Dec. 31, 2005, is likely not to be a smart tax move. In this case, your capital gain is short-term and taxed at ordinary income rates. Had you sold the same stock a few days later on Jan. 2, 2006, the gain would have been treated as long-term and taxed at the lower 15% or 5% rate, and in addition would be delayed another year.

Take Short-Term Losses

If you happen to have both short-term and long-term capital gains, you may want to consider realizing short-term capital losses on stocks you have held for less than one year. These short-term losses will offset your short-term gains, which are taxed at higher ordinary income rates. This will give you the most tax mileage for your capital loss.

Timing Capital Gains and Losses

When faced with large capital gains and losses, it may be advantageous for you to realize both in the same year. Suppose you have $30,000 of capital gains and $30,000 of capital losses. If you realize the gain in 2005, you will have to pay tax on the entire $30,000. If you decide to realize your loss in 2006, you'd have no capital gains to offset it, and you could only deduct $3,000 against your other income. The remaining $27,000 loss must be carried over into future years. Instead of delaying the tax benefits of your loss, you could choose to realize both the capital gain and loss in the same year. Since they completely offset each other, you would not owe any taxes.

On the other hand, if you do not have a large capital loss to offset, you should generally time the realization of long-term capital gains—which will be taxed at favorable rates—for years when you do not realize any capital losses. Then you can realize your future capital losses in years when you can immediately deduct them against other income that may be taxed at higher ordinary income rates.

The Bottom Line

As you can see, taxes can have a meaningful impact on your long-term investment performance. Investing in stocks without regard to the tax impact can greatly reduce your return. But by understanding the basic framework of investment taxation and using a few simple tax-planning strategies, you can work to maximize the only number that matters in the end: the amount of money that goes into your pocket.

Investor's Checklist

► Taxes are a fact of life, and tax ramifications are important to keep in mind when buying and selling stocks. With a few simple steps, you can greatly reduce the drag that taxes can have on returns.

► Long-term capital gains, or gains on the sale of assets such as stocks or bonds held for more than one year, are taxed at lower rates than ordinary income. Qualified dividends are also taxed at these lower rates. The current rates are 15% for many taxpayers, or 5% for taxpayers in the 10% or 15% income tax brackets.

► Capital losses can be used to offset capital gains. And to the extent capital losses exceed capital gains, up to $3,000 annually can be deducted against other income. However, keep in mind the wash sale rule.

► Deferring the payment of taxes can have a significant effect on your investment performance. When starting to invest in stocks, consider taking advantage of tax-deferred accounts such as 401(k)s and IRAs, and consider keeping turnover within your taxable accounts to a minimum.

► Waiting for long-term capital gain treatment and correctly timing the realization of capital gains and losses are simple strategies that will help you to be a more tax-efficient investor.

Quiz

1   Unless the provisions of the 2003 tax cut are extended, the lowered 15% and 10% tax rates for long-term capital gains and qualified dividends will expire in which year?

a	2009.
b	2018.
c	The 15% and 10% tax rates are permanent.

Answers to this quiz can be found on page 169

2   Which type of tax-advantaged account offers the potential for tax-exempt distributions?

a	401(k) account.
b	A traditional IRA.
c	A Roth IRA.

3   All other things being equal, which would you rather own in a taxable account?

a	Bonds.
b	The stock of a solid business that grows steadily over time but pays no dividend.
c	A high-yielding utility stock.

4   You must generally begin making mandatory withdrawals from 401(k) and traditional IRA accounts when you reach what age?

a	70 1/2.
b	59 1/2.
c	65.

5   When does your five-taxable-year period for Roth IRAs start?

a	On Jan. 1 of the tax year when you make your first contribution or conversion to a Roth IRA.
b	On the date of your first contribution or conversion into a Roth IRA.
c	On the date of your first withdrawal from a Roth IRA.

Worksheet

Answers to this worksheet can
be found on page 180

1   On Jan. 1, 2006, you purchase 100 shares of Microsoft for $30 a share and 200 shares of Intel
    for $25 a share. Suppose your income places you in the 15% income tax bracket. On July
    15, 2007, you sell your 100 shares of Microsoft for $40 a share. On June 10, 2008, you sell your
    200 shares of Intel for $50 a share. How much in capital gains tax do you owe from these
    two investments?

2   Assuming you are already investing, do you currently have any tax-advantaged accounts?
    If not, what types of accounts are available to lower your tax bill from investing?

3   Suppose you have $15,000 of unrealized capital gains and $10,000 of unrealized capital losses.
    How could you time the realization of your gains and losses to maximize your tax benefits?

Lesson 110: Using Financial Services Wisely

"Money frees you from doing things you dislike. Since I dislike doing nearly everything, money is handy."—Groucho Marx

Once you consider taxes and decide what type of investment account you'd like to open, the next nuts-and-bolts decision involves actually choosing a broker.

When thinking about a stockbroker, a picture of Charlie Sheen from the movie *Wall Street* often comes to mind. Thoughts of cold calls interrupting your dinner and pushy salesmen trying to sell the latest "hot stock" can scare investors away from buying stocks. In reality, however, it isn't so bad, and there are many options to choose from. In this lesson, we'll aim to provide the information you need to pick a broker who will help you reach your financial goals.

What Is a Broker?

Think of a broker as the middleman between you and the person you are buying your stock from or selling your stock to. When you place an order to either buy or sell a stock, your broker will find a party that is willing to take the other side of your transaction. Of course, the broker will charge a fee (commission) for this service. There are hundreds of brokers and other financial advisors, and they provide varying levels of service. For the purpose of this book, however, we'll focus on three types of service providers: full-service brokers, fee-based financial planners, and discount brokers.

Full-Service Brokers

Full-service brokers provide handholding through the investment process that often gives investors reassurance that they are not going it alone. They provide personalized service, as well as advice on what to buy and sell. This is the greatest benefit to full-service brokers, but the benefits can be outweighed by the costs—literally. This handholding does not come cheap, and the commissions charged by a full-service provider can quickly eat away at any investment gains your portfolio makes. It is difficult enough to achieve success at investing; we don't need another obstacle. We think investors would be well served to avoid these high fees if possible.

Another concern with full-service brokers is the inherent conflict of interest that drives many of the recommendations they give clients. Many brokers are compensated by trading activity, not performance. For example, most full-service brokers are paid based on a commission they receive for executing sales and purchases. So the more you trade, the more your broker will make. One of the reasons frequent trading is generally a bad idea is that it leads to higher commissions that will eat into your returns. It can also cause you to pay higher taxes on realized short-term capital gains.

So while it is against your best interest to trade often, a full-service broker has an incentive to encourage frequent trading, just to rake in the fees. At the end of the day, even the well-intentioned commission-based brokers face a conflict with your interests. If you decide to use a full-service broker, make sure to seek out those upstanding professionals who are willing to look beyond this conflict and put your interests ahead of their own.

Fee-Based Planners

If you still find the need for personalized, professional investment advice but want to avoid the conflicts of interest at full-service brokers, fee-based planners can be a worthy consideration. Fee-based planners usually charge their clients based on a variety of factors, and the way they get paid does not have a large inherent conflict of interest.

In general, planners and advisors get paid in one of three ways. First, they may charge you a percentage of your assets on an ongoing basis (say, 1% a year, not including brokerage costs or any expenses associated with mutual funds). Other planners charge a dollar rate on a per-job or hourly basis. Finally, others earn commissions on any products they sell you. Some planners may use a combination of these fee structures—for example, a planner might charge you an hourly rate to set up your plan and also put you in funds on which he or she earns a commission. The upshot is that most planners do not have the incentive to encourage frequent trading, but they can be just as (if not more) expensive as full-service brokers.

Discount Brokers

To avoid the pitfalls of full-service brokers and the costs of fee-based planners, using a discount broker is often the best option. Discount brokers differ from their full-service counterparts in that they offer bare-bones brokerage services, and typically do not offer advice. Investors with discount brokers don't have to worry about aggressive sales tactics or the conflicts of interest we discussed above. Instead, discount brokers such as Charles Schwab, E*Trade, and Ameritrade allow investors to make their own decisions regarding what to invest in.

Most importantly, the commissions that investors pay to discount brokers are significantly cheaper than the commissions charged by full-service brokers. Whereas a full-service brokerage may charge a commission in the hundreds of dollars per trade, a discount broker's commissions are often a fraction of this. And with the advent of the Internet, Web-based discount brokers make it easier than ever for individuals to maintain their own stock portfolios. Although discount brokers make investing easier, picking which broker to use can be difficult. In the following sections, we'll tell you what to look for when choosing a discount broker.

Often, a discount broker will entice you to open an account by offering short-term perks such as "20 free trades." Be careful of such offers. There are usually time limits for these trades, and the commissions after the free trades may be high.

About Those Free Trades

The True Cost of Commissions

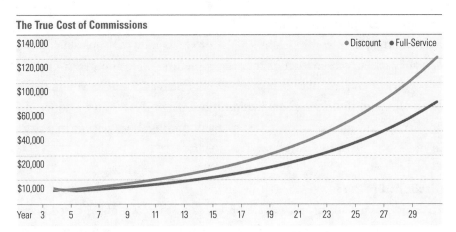

Consider two different accounts, each starting with $10,000, each receiving a 10% annual return, and each trades four times per year. The "discount" account pays $20 per trade, while the "full-service" account pays $80 per trade. As you can see, the difference in return over time is dramatic.

Costs

When looking for a discount broker, cost should be a major focal point. We've already established that discount brokers are significantly less expensive than full-service brokers, but there is a wide range of price options within the discount broker arena as well. For example, commissions can range anywhere from $30 to less than $10, depending on the broker. Obviously, the less you have to pay in commissions, the better. But there are also many other factors you should consider. Many brokers charge lower per-trade commissions for "active traders." For example, a brokerage house can require that investors make more than 20 or 30 trades a quarter or month before they qualify for the lower commissions. We've said it before and we'll say it again: All else equal, frequent trading will eat away at your returns over the long run.

Peripheral Services

Brokers sometimes charge higher commissions because they offer investors a variety of other useful services. For example, many brokerages offer third-party research for stocks. (Shameless plug: With a subscription to Morningstar. com's Premium Membership, you wouldn't need to worry about paying up for research. We have insightful independent Analyst Reports for more than 1,500 stocks.)

Although we think most investors are capable of making their own investment decisions, even the most experienced investors will eventually have a question or two about their accounts. This is why it's important to look for a broker that provides good customer service. Some companies have satellite offices in neighborhood strip malls, while others may provide 24-hour phone support. It's certainly worthwhile to look into a broker's customer service before making a decision.

Commissions aren't the only costs a broker can charge investors. Many brokerages can levy relatively large inactivity fees on accounts that do not trade a certain amount within a specified time frame. Inactivity fees can often sneak up on investors, so it is important to understand a broker's policy on them.

Watch Those Inactivity Fees

A more recent trend is for brokers to also provide other financial services, such as retail banking (checking and savings accounts) and loans. These services may be attractive for those looking for a "one-stop shop" for all their financial needs. The range of these services can vary, but they are also worth looking into.

After you've opened an account with your broker of choice, you have a variety of investing options and strategies at your fingertips. At Morningstar, we believe that a long-term investing strategy is the best way to achieve financial success, but it is important to understand some of the mechanics and options involved in trading and investing in stocks.

Making Trades

Investors can trade stocks through a broker using several methods, some of which offer them more control or the opportunity to juice their returns—with added risk, of course.

Market and Limit Orders

Placing an order to buy or sell shares of a company is relatively straightforward. There are various methods you can use, however, if you want to execute a trade at a specific price.

A market order is the most straightforward method of placing a trade. A market order tells the broker to buy or sell at the best price he or she can get in the market, and the trades are usually executed immediately. Since we recommend a long-term investing philosophy, fretting over a few pennies here and there doesn't make sense to us, and a market order is best in most cases.

A limit order means you can set the maximum price you are willing to pay for a stock, or a minimum price you'd be willing to sell a stock for. If the stock is trading anywhere below your maximum purchase price, or above the minimum selling price, the trade will be executed. However, because there are limitations when a limit order is placed, the trade might not be executed immediately. Also, some brokers charge extra when a limit order is requested.

Buying on Margin

Buying on margin is a risky way to pump up the potential return on your investment. Margin trades involve borrowing money from your broker to purchase an investment. Let's run through an example of how buying on margin can be profitable and also how it can be a risky game:

Let's say you want to buy 100 shares of fictional company Illini Basketballs Inc. Each share costs $10, so your total cost would be $1,000 (we'll ignore commissions for now). If those shares go up to $12 after you buy, your return would be 20%, or $200 (100 shares x $2 per share profit).

Now let's say you bought those 100 shares on margin. Instead of using $1,000 of your own money, you borrow $500 and use only $500 of your own money. Now if the stock goes up to $12, your return jumps to 40% ($200 profit/$500 initial investment).

Of course nothing is free, so you'd have to pay interest on the $500 you borrowed. Nevertheless, it's easy to see how buying shares of a company on margin can really juice your returns. But below is an example of how buying on margin can turn ugly. We'll use the same example as above, but with a twist:

You've borrowed $500 and used $500 of your own money to buy 100 shares of Illini Basketballs Inc. at $10. If Illini's shares drop to $8, you've suddenly lost 40% of your investment, and you still owe your broker the $500 it lent you.

If stock bought on margin keeps going down, you might even eventually get a dreaded "margin call." This means your broker is getting nervous that you might not have enough money to pay back the loan. If you get a margin call, you'd have to contribute more cash to your account, or sell some of your stocks to reduce your loan. Typically, these sales happen at precisely the wrong time—when stocks are down and at bargain-basement prices. Brokerage houses usually have set requirements that dictate how much of your own cash you need to have in your portfolio when trading on margin. Buying on margin is not for beginners, so tread carefully.

Shorting

It may sound funny, but investors can actually profit when a stock goes down in price. Shorting stocks involves selling borrowed shares with the intent of repurchasing them at a lower price. Instead of trying to buy low and sell high, you are simply reversing the order. Once again, let's go through an example:

You've been tracking fictional company Badgers Bricks Corp. and think its newest products are going to flop. The company is already on the ropes financially, and you think that this may be the last straw. You decide to short 100 shares of the company. After an order to short Badgers Bricks Corp.'s stock is placed, your broker will find 100 shares that it can lend to you. You immediately sell those shares on the marketplace for $10 and receive proceeds of $1,000. If the stock drops to $8, you can buy the shares for $800 and return them to your broker. Your profit is $200 ($1,000 minus $800).

This sounds easy enough, but no investment is foolproof. If you make the wrong bet when shorting a stock, your downside is potentially unlimited. In a best-case scenario, the stock you short will go down to $0 and your profit equals all the cash you received from selling the borrowed shares. On the downside, the stock you short could increase in price, and there is no limit on how high it could go. Remember, those shares are borrowed and eventually will have to be returned. If the price keeps going up, you'll be stuck paying a lot more to buy the stock back, perhaps much more than you could have made if the stock went to zero. The important thing to remember is that the potential downside in shorting stocks is unlimited. As with buying on margin, be careful.

Four Ideas to Keep Costs Low

As we've shown in this lesson and the one before it, taxes and commissions can eat into your returns if you are not careful. To minimize the frictional costs of stock investing, consider doing the following:

1. Make use of tax-advantaged accounts, such as IRAs and 401(k)s, to shield your investment income from taxes.

2. Try to use the most inexpensive broker possible; minimize the per-trade fees you have to pay.

3. Do not be tempted to trade too often. You will not only rack up commission expenses, but you will also likely increase your tax bill.

4. To minimize your annual tax bill, plan to realize capital gains and losses at the most opportune times.

The Bottom Line

The mechanics of trading are really not very difficult to grasp. But to be a successful investor, it is certainly worthwhile to use financial services wisely by paying attention to fees and commissions, which will inevitably eat into your returns. Minimizing your fees, like minimizing your taxes, is an extremely worthwhile endeavor.

Investor's Checklist

▶ For individual investors willing to make their own investment decisions, discount brokers are generally far superior to full-service brokers. Discount brokers charge reasonable commissions and come without the conflicts of interest found at full-service brokerage houses.

▶ If you still want advice from a professional investment advisor, your interests will be more aligned with your advisor's if you pay via flat-rate fees rather than via commissions. If you do choose a full-service broker, make sure it is one that puts your interests first.

▶ Limit orders are ways to specify the minimum and maximum prices at which you wish to have a trade executed.

▶ Shorting stocks and buying stocks on margin are two risky investing strategies. Shorting stocks is a way to bet that a stock price will decrease, and buying on margin involves borrowing money to buy shares of a company. Buying on margin will amplify your returns, whether those returns are positive or negative.

Quiz

Answers to this quiz can be found on page 170

1   Say you buy 100 shares of fictional company Hawkeye's Footballs, Inc., on margin for $100 per share. You borrow 50% of the funds used for the purchase. If the stock price increases to $110, what would your return on investment be? (Ignore commissions and interest costs.)

a	10%.
b	40%.
c	20%.

2   What is a broker?

a	The person who does your taxes.
b	A middleman between you and the person you are buying your stock from or selling your stock to.
c	A journalist who writes about financial topics.

3   You short 100 shares of fictional company Hoosier Soybeans Corp. at $20. The shares subsequently drop to $15, and you sell. What would your cash profit be?

a	Minus $500.
b	$250.
c	$500.

4   If you place a market order to buy 100 shares of fictional company Wolverines Sailboats Corp., at what price and when would the trade be executed?

a	The trade would be executed immediately at the best available price.
b	The trade would be executed when the shares hit your specified buy price.
c	The trade would not be executed until the next day at the best price available.

5   Full-service brokers typically:

a	Get paid based on your investment performance and not your trading activity.
b	Provide a lot of personal attention and advice.
c	Charge low commissions.

Worksheet

1   Describe some of the differences between a discount and full-service broker.

Answers to this worksheet can be found on page 181

2   Explain why shorting stocks could be risky.

3   What is the difference between a market and limit order?

4   What are some of the factors you should consider before choosing a discount broker?

Lesson 111: Understanding the News

"It's amazing that the amount of news that happens in the world every day always just exactly fits the newspaper."—Jerry Seinfeld

"The Dow fell 71 points today..."
"The S&P 500 continued its recent climb..."
"ABC Company missed its quarterly earnings target..."
"XYZ Company's shares jumped $2 as a result of analyst upgrades..."

These are common statements you may hear on any given day as you flip past a financial news channel on your TV or scan the headlines in your newspaper. But what are the Dow and the S&P 500? What is the Nasdaq? What happens when a company misses earnings targets or gets upgraded or downgraded by analysts? What does any of this stuff mean to you, as an investor?

In this lesson, we are going to focus on building an understanding of some of the things you may typically hear in the financial news. Then we are going to learn how to separate what actually matters from what is nothing more than "noise."

Stock Indexes

A stock index is simply a grouping or a composite of a number of different stocks, often with similar characteristics. Stock indexes are typically used to discuss the overall performance of the stock market, in terms of changes in the market price of the stocks as well as how much trading activity there is in any particular period. Three of the most widely followed indexes are the Dow Jones Industrial Average, the S&P 500, and the Nasdaq Composite.

The Dow Jones Industrial Average

Known as just the "Dow" for short, this index is not really an average, nor does it exclusively track heavy industry anymore. The index is composed of 30 large stocks from a wide spectrum of industries. General Motors and General Electric are the only two companies that have been part of the Dow Jones Industrial Average since it was created in 1928. The latest change to the Dow was the addition of insurance company American International Group, pharmaceutical firm Pfizer, and telecommunications company Verizon in April 2004, while AT&T, Eastman Kodak, and International Paper were dropped to make room.

At the close of business on Jan. 1, 2005, the Dow stood at 10,783. How is this figure calculated?

The index is calculated by taking the 30 stocks in the average, adding up their prices, and dividing by a divisor. This divisor was originally equal to the number of stocks in the average (to give the average price of a stock), but this divisor has shrunk steadily over the years. It dropped below one in 1986 and was equal to 0.135 in January 2005. This shrinkage is needed to offset arbitrary events such as stock splits and changes in the roster of companies. With the divisor at 0.135, the effect is to multiply the sum of the prices by about 7.4. (The numeral one divided by 0.135 is approximately 7.4.) To look at it another way, each dollar of price change in any of the 30 Dow stocks represents a roughly 7.4-point change in the Dow.

Because the Dow includes only 30 companies, one company can have much more influence on it than on more broad-based indexes. Also, since the prices of the 30 stocks are added and divided by the common denominator, stocks with larger prices have more weight in the index than stocks with lower prices. Thus, the Dow is a price-weighted index. It's also useful to remember that the 30 stocks that make up the Dow are picked by the editors of the *Wall Street Journal*, rather than by any quantitative criteria. The editors try to pick stocks that represent the market, but there's an inevitable element of subjectivity (and luck) in such a method.

Despite its narrower focus, the Dow tracks quite well with broader indexes such as the S&P 500 over the long run.

The 30 Companies in the Dow Jones Industrial Average

3M MMM	**Honeywell International** HON
Alcoa AA	**Intel** INTC
Altria Group MO	**International Business Machines** IBM
American Express AXP	**Johnson & Johnson** JNJ
American International Group AIG	**JPMorgan Chase & Co.** JPM
Boeing BA	**McDonald's** MCD
Caterpillar CAT	**Merck & Co.** MRK
Citigroup C	**Microsoft** MSFT
Coca-Cola KO	**Pfizer** PFE
E.I. DuPont de Nemours & Co. DD	**Procter & Gamble** PG
ExxonMobil XOM	**SBC Communications** SBC
General Electric GE	**United Technologies** UTX
General Motors GM	**Verizon Communications** VZ
Hewlett-Packard HPQ	**Wal-Mart Stores** WMT
Home Depot HD	**Walt Disney** DIS

As of May 2005

The S&P 500

The Dow Jones Industrial Average usually gets most of the attention, but the S&P 500 Index is much more important to the investment world. Index funds that track the S&P 500 hold hundreds of billions of dollars, and thousands of fund managers and other financial professionals track their performance against this ubiquitous index. But what exactly is the S&P 500, anyway?

The Standard & Poor's 500 as we know it today came into being on March 4, 1957. The makers of that first index retroactively figured its value going back to 1926, and they decided to use an arbitrary base value of 10 for the average value of the index during the years 1941 through 1943. This meant that in 1957 the index stood at about 45, which was also the average price of a share of stock. The companies in the original s&p 500 accounted for about 90% of the value of the u.s. stock market, but this percentage has shrunk to just more than 80% today as the number of stocks being traded has expanded.

Although it's usually referred to as a large-cap index, the s&p 500 does not just consist of the 500 largest companies in the u.s. The companies in the index are chosen by a committee at investment company Standard & Poor's. The committee meets monthly to discuss possible changes to the list and chooses companies on the basis of "market size, liquidity, and group representation." New members are added to the 500 only when others drop out because of mergers or (less commonly) a faltering business.

Some types of stocks are explicitly excluded from the index, including real estate stocks and companies that primarily hold stock in other companies. For example, Berkshire Hathaway, the holding company of Warren Buffett, arguably the world's greatest investor, isn't included, despite having one of the largest market values of all u.s. companies. Also, the index is composed exclusively of u.s. companies today.

Size matters with the s&p 500. Because the companies chosen for the index tend to be leaders in their industries, most are large firms. But the largest of the large-capitalization stocks have a much greater effect on the s&p 500 than the smaller companies do. That's because the index is market-cap-weighted, so that a company's influence on the index is proportional to its size. (Remember, a company's market cap is determined by multiplying the number of shares outstanding by the price for each share.) Thus, General Electric and ExxonMobil, with the two biggest market caps among U.S. companies, accounted for 3.4% and 2.9%, respectively, of the S&P 500 as of the beginning of 2005. In contrast, other smaller companies can account for less than 0.1% of the index.

The Nasdaq Composite

The Nasdaq Composite was formed in 1971 and includes the stocks of more than 3,000 companies today. It includes stocks that are listed on the technology-company-heavy Nasdaq stock exchange, one of the market's largest exchanges. (Other major stock exchanges include the New York Stock Exchange, or the NYSE, and the American Stock Exchange, or AMEX.) Like the S&P 500, the Nasdaq is a market-cap-weighted index. For a stock to be included in the Nasdaq Composite, it must trade on the Nasdaq stock exchange and meet other specific criteria. If a company fails to meet all of the criteria at any time, it is then removed from the composite.

"Noise" Versus News

Anyone interested in keeping up with current business events has plenty of opportunity. Walk into any newsstand, and you'll see all kinds of newspapers and magazine titles dedicated to the business world. Cable television offers several business news channels. And the Internet provides countless business and financial Web sites.

Oftentimes, events in the news cause stock prices to move both up and down, sometimes dramatically. Sometimes the market's reaction to the headlines is warranted; many other times, it's not. For an investor, the real challenge is deciphering all of the headlines and stories to determine what is really relevant for your stocks.

Here at Morningstar, we practice the discipline of scouting out great companies with long-term competitive advantages that we expect will create shareholder value for the foreseeable future. Then we wait until their stocks become cheap before investing in them for the long haul. In keeping a watchful eye out for solid investment opportunities, we constantly monitor and evaluate the ever-changing business environment. As we digest the events that affect any given company, we continually ask ourselves, "Does this information affect the long-term competitive advantages and resulting cash flow of this company? Does it change the stock's long-term investing prospects?"

This is key to understanding the investment process. Periodically, news will break that does not affect a company's long-term competitive advantages, but its stock price will fall anyway. This may lead to a buying opportunity. Remember, "Mr. Market" tends to be quite temperamental, and not always rightfully so.

Noise or News?   If a piece of news does not impact a company's cash flow, it is likely noise. If it does impact cash flow, it is probably worthwhile to pay attention.

Negative Earnings Surprises. Wall Street is full of professionals whose job is to analyze companies and provide opinions about them and estimates about their future financial results. While most of them are very intelligent individuals who have a wealth of information and experience, they tend to be much too shortsighted. These analysts typically will come up with "earnings estimates" for the upcoming three-month period. If a company's actual results fall short of analysts' expectations, this is known as a "negative earnings surprise." On such disappointing news, the company's stock price may fall. (Conversely, if a company performs better than what analysts expect, it will have a "positive earnings surprise," which may cause the stock price to increase.)

Let's pretend that Wal-Mart announced earnings that fell short of analysts' estimates by a measly two cents a share because it didn't sell as many widgets during the holiday season as people expected. Let's also assume that the stock fell on the disappointment. Does this disappointing shopping season mean that Wal-Mart's long-term competitive advantages have been eroded? Probably not. Wal-Mart remains the largest retailer in the world, with great economies of scale and a remarkable distribution network, which allows the company to pass huge cost savings on to customers, which, in turn, keeps customers coming back. So it fell slightly below analysts' estimates in one particular quarter…big deal!

Analyst Upgrades/Downgrades. In addition to providing estimates of what they think a company's sales and earnings will be, Wall Street analysts also provide recommendations for stocks they cover, such as "Buy," "Hold," or "Sell." When an analyst changes his or her rating for a company's stock, the stock price often moves in the direction of the change. Does this upgrade or downgrade affect the business prospects of the company? No, the opinion of one person does not alter the intrinsic value of the firm, which is determined by the company's cash flows. But maybe the analyst made the change because he or she thought the company's business prospects have deteriorated. Maybe that's right, maybe not. Check it out, and decide for yourself.

Newsworthy Events. Other times investors will hear about events that have them running for cover, and rightfully so. One such event is the announcement of a regulatory investigation by an organization such as the Securities and Exchange Commission or the Department of Justice. While such announcements by themselves by no means predict impending doom, who knows what nasty surprises may lurk for investors as regulators start turning over rocks? Plenty of investors have been burned badly by the results of such investigations—just ask the shareholders of Enron, Tyco, or WorldCom.

Another item to be wary of is a significant lawsuit. Corporate litigation is almost everywhere you look (these days, it's almost a normal part of doing business), and estimates of any significant legal damage are usually already priced into a stock. However, lawsuits often attract others, which could place very large uncertainties on a company's performance.

A great example of how such legal issues can affect the true value of a company is occurring at the time of this writing. Bellwether drug manufacturer Merck is experiencing a double-whammy related to litigation. Vioxx, Merck's arthritis-pain-relieving drug that was once perceived as a blockbuster, has been linked to heart problems in patients taking it. The company had to recall Vioxx from the market, and it is facing serious legal liabilities. Shortly thereafter, a court ruling shortened the patent life on Merck's number-two-selling drug Fosamax, meaning competitors can introduce a substitute much quicker than previously thought. Both situations have the ability to seriously reduce Merck's future cash flows.

The Bottom Line

Successful investing requires you to keep a steady hand. Your patience and willpower will get regularly tested as the stock market reacts to news, sometimes justifiably, other times not. Just remember that not every bump in the road is the edge of a cliff. If you react by racing to sell your stocks on every little piece of bad news, you will find yourself trading far too frequently (with the requisite taxes and commissions), and often selling at the worst possible time. But by using focused discipline in separating the news that matters from the noise that doesn't, you should emerge with satisfactory investment results.

Investor's Checklist

► Stock market indexes are used as a barometer to gauge the health of the overall stock market or stocks with similar characteristics, such as size or industry. Different indexes are calculated in different ways.

► Events in the news often cause a stock's price to move up or down, sometimes dramatically. However, not all news events regarding a particular company should affect your investing decisions.

► When assessing a company's current happenings, constantly ask yourself, "Does this information affect the company's long-term competitive advantages and cash flow? Does it change the stock's long-term prospects?"

► On face value, earnings surprises and analyst revisions do not affect a company's long-term competitive advantages or investment prospects. News items to heed include regulatory investigations and significant lawsuits.

Quiz

Answers to this quiz can be found on page 170

1   The divisor used to calculate the Dow:

a	Has been constant.
b	Has been shrinking steadily in recent years.
c	Has been rising steadily in recent years.

2   Which one of the following three companies is a member of the S&P 500?

a	Software giant Microsoft.
b	Warren Buffett's holding company Berkshire Hathaway.
c	Dutch oil giant Royal Dutch Petroleum.

3   Which of the following stock indexes is price-weighted?

a	Dow Jones Industrial Average.
b	Nasdaq Composite Index.
c	S&P 500 Index.

4   If a company's actual earnings results are different than what analysts expect, this is known as:

a	An analyst revision.
b	An earnings surprise.
c	A stock split.

5   Which of the following would most likely affect a company's long-term investment outlook?

a	The company missed analyst estimates by a penny.
b	The company's stock was recently downgraded by a Wall Street analyst from "Buy" to "Hold."
c	The SEC is investigating the company to determine if it fraudulently misstated its financial results for the past several years.

Worksheet

1   Assume the current divisor used in calculating the Dow is 0.125. By how many points would the index change if one of the stocks in the Dow increased by a dollar while the rest remained flat? What if two stocks in the Dow each fell a dollar, a third fell $5, and the rest were unchanged?

Answers to this worksheet can be found on page 181

2   Why do you think there are initial stock price movements after an earnings surprise or analyst revision?

3   Can you think of some other examples of headlines or news events that would be considered "noise"? What about some other examples that would have an impact on your long-term investment?

Lesson 112: Start Thinking Like an Analyst

"In business, I look for economic castles protected by unbreachable 'moats.'"
—Warren Buffett

Investing is far more than just learning basic accounting and crunching numbers; it is also about observing the world around us. It is about recognizing trends and what those trends will ultimately mean in terms of dollars.

Thinking like an analyst can help because it can provide some organized ways in which to observe the world. We all have analytical skills, but the degree to which these skills are developed depends on the individual. Honing your analytical skills can help you organize some of the information that overwhelms you each day.

For example, it's hard not to notice how fast food restaurants are all located near one another. Maybe this is an obvious question, but why is that? Clearly those restaurants located at the only exit for 50 miles in the middle of Kansas don't have much choice, and certainly business and residential zoning regulations dictate locations to some extent. But why do all of the quick-service restaurants locate near one another when alternatives are available? After all, what good does it do for some of these restaurants to be located in clusters? What happens to McDonald's if Wendy's is right next door?

Four Basic Questions

The answers to these questions for restaurants, or for any business, can be found by asking four very general questions to kick-start the analyst thought process:

1. What is the goal of the business?
2. How does the business make money?
3. How well is the business actually doing?
4. How well is the business positioned relative to its competitors?

Once you start thinking in these terms, and sharpen your observational skills, you'll be well on your way to thinking like an analyst, constantly on the hunt for investment opportunities.

The goal of restaurants, for example, is to feed customers. This seems pretty straightforward—although some restaurants have also tried to combine meals with entertainment to mixed success—but don't just assume a business's purpose is obvious. Be sure you have a good idea of what it's really trying to achieve. Then ask if it makes sense for this business to try to achieve this objective. Does it make sense for a restaurant to also entertain customers, for example?

Once you have a good idea of what the business is trying to do, think about how it makes money. In our restaurant example, how much does the food in the restaurant actually cost? Can the restaurant charge more for its food because of a pleasant ambiance or because it is providing entertainment? Is the restaurant trying to sell a lot of meals at a low price, or is it attempting to sell fewer meals but at a much higher profit per meal?

Then ask yourself, "How well is the business doing?" Don't worry about picking up any financial statements just yet; rather, focus on observing what you can about the business. Back to our restaurant example, think about where you choose to eat and why. Has your favorite place been around a long time? Are there lots of locations for your favorite restaurant? Are they busy, with people in line or in the parking lot? Are they in good locations? Do they seem to get a lot of repeat business? Do they seem to have a better caliber of wait staff? How fancy are the interiors? As a potential investor in this or similar businesses, all this stuff counts.

If you think you have a pretty good understanding of the business's performance, at least as an observer, spend some time thinking about how well it functions in its industry. In other words, assess the competition.

Is there a lot of competition in its industry? With restaurants, there certainly seem to be a lot of choices, but what about an entirely different industry, like computers? Are there as many types of computer companies as there are restaurants? Not by a long shot. Does that mean that the computer industry isn't as competitive as the restaurant industry? Not necessarily. Instead it might mean that competition functions very differently. Since it takes a ton of capital to start up a computer company, and not so much to start up a restaurant, maybe there is more risk in computer manufacturing? Maybe finding new products is also more difficult? Maybe one of the only ways to compete in the industry is on price? Asking these kinds of questions can give you a good idea of how well a specific business is positioned to cope with the challenges it may encounter.

At this point it may seem like we're going a little nuts generating questions, but thinking like an analyst involves observing the business world and asking questions to understand how it works. Thankfully, there are also experts who have done a lot of this thinking already, and many of them have developed useful frameworks to help organize our thinking even more.

If we think back on the four questions we mentioned earlier, we should be able to get a good handle on a business's goals and on its performance just by reading about it and studying its financial statements. It's really the last question, the one in which we consider how well a company is positioned relative to its competitors, where we might need some more help.

Finding a Framework: Moats

It's a bit strange to think that an image typically associated with England and the Middle Ages might offer a framework for stock analysis. As we've already seen, in order to really think like an analyst, it's important to consider factors beyond just the numbers. After all, our quest is to find exceptional companies delivering outstanding performance, in which case we may need to put forth extra effort to find that "Holy Grail."

One helpful concept is that of an "economic moat." And while you may not hear it used as often as terms such as P/E ratio or operating profit, the concept of an economic moat is a guiding principle in Morningstar's stock analysis and valuation. Eventually the idea may gain more of a following since we think it is the foundation for identifying companies that create shareholder value over the long term. In the meantime, we'll just consider ourselves lucky to have a framework that can separate really great companies from the merely good ones.

What Is an Economic Moat?

Quite simply, an economic moat is a long-term competitive advantage that allows a company to earn oversized profits over time. The term was coined by one of our favorite investors of all time, Warren Buffet, who realized that companies that reward investors over the long term have a durable competitive advantage. Assessing that advantage involves understanding what kind of defense, or competitive barrier, the company has been able to build for itself in its industry.

Moats are important from an investment perspective because any time a company develops a useful product or service, it isn't long before other firms try to capitalize on that opportunity by producing a similar—if not better—product. Basic economic theory says that in a perfectly competitive market, rivals will eventually eat up any excess profits earned by a successful business. In other words, competition makes it difficult for most firms to generate strong growth and profits over an extended period of time since any advantage is always at risk of imitation.

The strength and sustainability of a company's economic moat will determine whether the firm will be able to prevent a competitor from taking business away or eroding its earnings. In our view, companies with wide economic moats are best positioned to keep competitors at bay over the long term, but we also use the terms "narrow" and "none" to describe a company's moat. We don't often talk about the depth of a moat, yet it's a good way of thinking about how much money a company can make with its advantage.

To determine whether or not a company has an economic moat, follow these four steps:

1. Evaluate the firm's historical profitability. Has the firm been able to generate a solid return on its assets and on shareholder equity? This is probably the most important component to identifying whether or not a company has a moat. While much about assessing a moat is qualitative, the bedrock of analyzing a company still relies on solid financial metrics.

ROA and ROE

Return on assets (ROA) and return on equity (ROE) are two different ways to quantify a company's profitability, and they are also excellent ways to determine if a company has a moat or not.
We will describe how to calculate these ratios in much greater detail in Workbook #2, but the basic, boiled-down calculations are as follows:

$$\text{ROA} = \frac{\text{Net Income}}{\text{Total Assets}} \qquad \text{ROE} = \frac{\text{Net Income}}{\text{Shareholder Equity}}$$

Typically, companies with economic moats will have double-digit returns on both measures over a number of years.

---

2. Assuming that the firm has solid returns on its capital and is consistently profitable, try to identify the source of those profits. Is the source an advantage that only this company has, or is it one that other companies can easily imitate? The harder it is for a rival to imitate an advantage, the more likely the company has a barrier in its industry and a source of economic profit.

3. Estimate how long the company will be able to keep competitors at bay. We refer to this time period as the company's competitive advantage period, and it can be as short as several months or as long as several decades. The longer the competitive advantage period, the wider the economic moat.

4. Think about the industry's competitive structure. Does it have many profitable firms or is it hypercompetitive with only a few companies scrounging for the last dollar? Highly competitive industries will likely offer less attractive profit growth over the long haul.

Types of Economic Moats

After researching thousands of companies, we've identified four main types of economic moats.

Low-Cost Producer. Companies that can deliver their goods or services at a low cost, typically due to economies of scale, have a distinct competitive advantage because they can undercut their rivals on price.

Wal-Mart is a great example of a low-cost producer, and its low costs allow it to price its products the most attractively. As a dominant player in retailing, the company's size provides it with enormous scale efficiencies, or operating leverage, that it uses to keep costs low. Scale allows Wal-Mart to do its own purchasing more efficiently since it has roughly 5,000 large stores worldwide, and it gives the company tremendous bargaining power with its suppliers. Since the company positions itself as a low-cost retailer, it wants to ensure it gives the lowest prices to its customers. This can translate into tough bargaining terms for those firms that want to sell their products on Wal-Mart's shelves. As a result, Wal-Mart is able to offer prices that competitors have a difficult time matching—one reason why you don't see too many Kmarts around anymore.

High Switching Costs. Switching costs are those one-time inconveniences or expenses a customer incurs in order to switch over from one product to another. If you've ever taken the time to move all of your account information from one bank to another, you know what a hassle it can be—so there would have to be a really good reason, like a package deal on an account and mortgage for example, for you to consider switching again.

Companies aim to create high switching costs in order to "lock in" customers. The more customers are locked in, the more likely a company can pass along added costs to them without risking customer loss to a competitor.

Surgeons encounter these switching costs when they train to do procedures using specific medical devices, such as the artificial joint products from medical-device companies Biomet or Stryker. After training to learn to use a specific product, switching to another would require the surgeon to forgo comfort and familiarity—and what patient, much less surgeon, would want that? Additionally, because the surgeon would have to be trained to use a new, competing product, he or she would also have to contend with lost time and money resulting from not performing as many surgical procedures. Clearly, with certain products and services, the switching costs can be quite high.

The Network Effect. The network effect is one of the most powerful competitive advantages, and it is also one of the easiest to spot. The network effect occurs when the value of a particular good or service increases for both new and existing users as more people use that good or service.

For example, the fact that there are literally millions of people using eBay makes the company's service incredibly valuable and all but impossible for another company to duplicate. For anyone wanting to sell something online via an auction, eBay provides the most potential buyers and is the most attractive. Meanwhile, for buyers, eBay has the widest selection. This advantage feeds on itself, and eBay's strength only increases as more users sign on.

Intangible Assets. Some companies have an advantage over competitors because of unique nonphysical, or "intangible," assets. Intangibles are things such as intellectual property rights (patents, trademarks, and copyrights), government approvals, brand names, a unique company culture, or a geographic advantage.

In some cases, whole industries derive huge benefits from intangible assets. Consumer-products manufacturers are one example. They build profits on the power of brands to distinguish their products. Well-known PepsiCo is a leader in salty snacks and sports drinks, and the firm boasts a lineup of strong brands, innovative products, and an impressive distribution network. The company's investment in advertising and marketing distinguishes its products on store shelves and allows PepsiCo to command premium prices. Consumers will pay more for a bag of Frito-Lay chips than for a bag of generic chips. As the value of a brand increases, the manufacturer is also often able to be more demanding in its distribution relationships. To a large degree, brand power creates demand for those chips and secures their placement on store shelves.

One final thought about economic moats: It is possible for some companies to have more than one type of moat. For example, many companies that use the network effect also benefit from economies of scale, because these companies tend to grow so large that they dwarf smaller competitors. In general, the more types of economic moat a company has—and the wider those moats are—the better.

20 Wide-Moat Companies

Stock Name	Low-Cost Producer	High Customer Switching Costs	Network Effect	Intangible Assets
Adobe Systems ADBE		■	■	
Amazon.com AMZN	■			■
American Express AXP		■	■	
Automatic Data Processing ADP		■		
Berkshire Hathaway BRK.B				■
Chicago Mercantile Exchange CME		■	■	
Citigroup C		■		
Coca-Cola KO				■
Dell DELL	■			
Dow Jones & Co. DJ				■
eBay EBAY		■	■	
ExxonMobil XOM	■			
Harley-Davidson HDI				■
Intel INTC	■			■
Intuit INTU		■		■
Kinder Morgan KMI		■		
Microsoft MSFT		■	■	■
PepsiCo PEP				■
Pfizer PFE				■
Wal-Mart WMT	■			

The Bottom Line

Successful long-term investing involves more than just identifying solid businesses, or finding businesses that are growing rapidly, or buying cheap stocks. We believe that successful investing also involves evaluating whether a business will stand the test of time.

Moats are a useful framework to help answer this question. Identifying a moat will take a little more effort than looking up a few numbers, but we think understanding a company's competitive position is an important process for determining its long-term profitability. And as we stated earlier in this book, how well a company's stock performs is directly related to the profits the firm can generate over the long haul.

Investor's Checklist

▶ Investing is as much a qualitative exercise as a quantitative one. Being a great investor involves observing and thinking about the world around us.

▶ To begin to think like an analyst, ask yourself the following questions about any business you are considering:
What is the goal of the business?
How does the business make money?
How well is the business actually doing?
How well is the business positioned relative to its competitors?

▶ The most profitable companies tend to become less profitable over time as competitors quickly seek out similar opportunities. Great companies maintain strong profitability over a long period of time.

▶ An economic moat is a long-term competitive advantage allowing a company to earn oversized profits over time.

▶ The four main ways a company can create an economic moat are:
1. Being a low-cost producer.
2. Benefiting from high switching costs.
3. Having a network effect.
4. Owning intangible assets.

Quiz

1   Why might a restaurant company be unlikely to ever have anything more than a narrow moat?

a	Because consumer switching costs are so low.
b	Because labor costs are so high restaurants can never be profitable.
c	Because of the amount of money restaurants need to invest in branding.

Answers to this quiz can be found on page 171

2   Why are economic moats advantageous?

a	They allow a company to generate profits and keep competitors at bay.
b	They help a company improve its brand.
c	They help make sure a company's CEO isn't too shallow.

3   High switching costs help companies:

a	Develop new products.
b	Attract new customers.
c	Raise prices without the risk of losing customers.

4   Which of these is not a type of economic moat?

a	Low-cost producer.
b	Technological expertise.
c	Network effect.

5   Which of these companies best exemplifies the use of the network effect?

a	Best Buy.
b	eBay.
c	Southwest Airlines.

Worksheet

Answers to this worksheet can be found on page 182

1   Consider a business that interests you. Answer the following questions for this business:

What is the goal of the business?

How does the business make money?

How well is the business actually doing?

How well is the business positioned relative to its competitors?

2   Write down the four types of economic moats. These are worth remembering.

3   What, other than eBay, is a good example of a company that benefits from a network effect moat?

4   How does determining economic moats help investors?

Lesson 113: Using Morningstar's Ratings for Stocks

"What is a cynic? A man who knows the price of everything and the value of nothing."—Oscar Wilde

It's amazing how much attention some people pay to stock quotes, and how little they pay to the value of the underlying businesses they are buying. At Morningstar, we evaluate stocks as pieces of a business and not as "little wiggling things with charts attached." We believe that purchasing shares of superior businesses at discounts to their fair values, and allowing those businesses to compound value over long periods of time, is the surest way to create wealth in the stock market.

The market may not always agree with our long-term investment philosophy, so sometimes our recommendations are out of step with consensus thinking. When stocks are high and richly valued, relatively few will receive the highest Morningstar Rating of 5 stars. But when the market tumbles, there will be many more 5-star stocks. We think good companies are more attractive when they are cheap than when they are expensive, so we find fewer opportunities when the market is overheating. If we wait to buy clothes and flat-panel televisions until they go on sale, why shouldn't we also purchase stocks at bargain prices?

Legendary stock investor Warren Buffett highlighted the importance of treating stocks as companies and not as "little wiggling things with charts attached." We will talk much more about Warren Buffett in later workbooks in this series.

More than a Squiggly Line

Morningstar has been analyzing investment strategies for nearly 20 years, and we have become experts at separating successful styles from the mediocre majority. In this lesson, we will share our approach to rating stocks so that you have an opportunity to benefit from our investment strategy and build enduring wealth in the market.

145

What Is Fair Value?

Most any investment, whether it's buying a home or purchasing a stock, boils down to an initial outlay followed by (hopefully) a stream of future income. The trick is deciding on a fair price to pay for that expected stream of future income.

Let's say a stock trades at $20 per share. If you crunch the numbers—projected sales growth, future profit margins, and so on—you might estimate the stock's fair price per share to be $30. You pay $20 for the stock, and in return you receive a stream of income valued at $30. That's a great deal. If the stock was trading at $40, above the $30 fair value of the future income stream, you are looking at an expensive stock.

Estimating a fair value is no trivial task. As such, we devote several lessons to this topic in the next workbook of this series.

At Morningstar, our analysts estimate a company's fair value by determining how much we would pay today for all the streams of excess cash generated by the company in the future. We arrive at this value by forecasting a company's future financial performance using a detailed discounted cash-flow model that factors in projections for the company's income statement, balance sheet, and cash-flow statement. The result is an analyst-driven estimate of the stock's fair value.

Different Investments, Different Star Ratings

The Morningstar Rating for stocks is different than the Morningstar Rating for funds. The Morningstar Rating for funds describes how well a fund has balanced return and risk (or volatility) in the past. The Morningstar Rating for stocks uses projections of a company's future operating performance to estimate whether the stock is overvalued or undervalued.

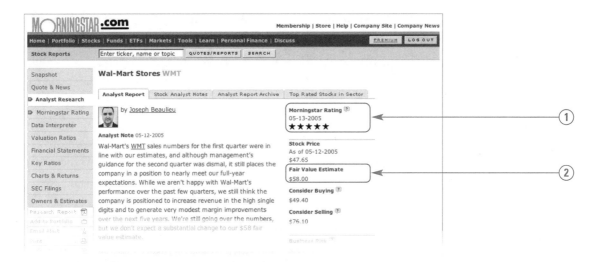

The Morningstar Rating (star rating) and fair value estimate are at the top of each Analyst Report for the nearly 1,600 companies we currently cover.

How Do We Assign Stars?

The Morningstar Rating is based on a stock's market price relative to its esti-mated fair value, adjusted for risk. Generally speaking, stocks trading at large discounts to our analysts' fair value estimates will receive higher (4 or 5) star ratings, and stocks trading at large premiums to their fair value estimates will receive lower (1 or 2) star ratings. Stocks that are trading very close to our analysts' fair value estimates will usually get 3-star ratings.

Not all companies are created equal. As such, the discount required to our fair value estimate to get to 5 stars increases as the quality of a company decreases. We require smaller discounts for high-quality businesses because we are more confident about our cash-flow projections and in their fair val-ues. The future is inherently uncertain, and that uncertainty is greater for some companies than others. Accordingly, we require larger discounts to our fair value for riskier or uncertain businesses.

When investing in any asset, you should expect a return that adequately compensates you for the risks inherent in the investment. Assuming that the stock's market price and fair value eventually converge, 3-star stocks should offer a "fair return." A fair return is one that adequately compensates you for the riskiness of the stock. Put another way, 3-star stocks should offer investors a return that's roughly equal to the stock's cost of equity. The cost of equity is often called the "required return" because it represents the return an investor requires for taking on the risk of owning a stock.

Fair Value Versus Price Target	The Morningstar fair value estimate is not the same as a price target. There is a key difference between the two prices: The Morningstar fair value is based on how much we think the stock is worth, while a target price often estimates how much other investors are willing to pay for the stock. This divergence emerges because we at Morningstar tend to assess stocks differently than Wall Street typically evaluates them.

On the other hand, 5-star stocks should offer an investor a return that's well above the company's cost of equity. High-risk, 5-star stocks should also offer a better expected return than low-risk, 5-star stocks. Conversely, low-rated stocks have significantly lower expected returns. If a stock drops to 1 star, that means we expect it to lose money for investors based on our assessment of the stock's fair value.

It is important to remember that if a stock's market price is significantly above our fair value estimate, it will receive a lower star rating, no matter how wonderful we think the business or its management is. Even the best company is a poor investment if an investor overpays for its shares.

What Causes a Star Rating to Change?

Morningstar's stock star ratings are updated daily, and therefore they can change daily. The ratings can change because of a move in the stock's price, a change in the analyst's estimate of the stock's fair value, a change in the analyst's assessment of a company's business risk, or a combination of any of these factors. The Morningstar Rating for stocks includes a small buffer around the cutoff between each rating to reduce the number of rating changes produced by random market "noise." If a $50 stock moves up and down by $0.25 each day over a few days, the buffer will prevent the star rating from changing each day based on this insignificant change.

It is important to note that our fair value estimates do not change very often, but the market prices do. Therefore, stocks often gain or lose stars based just on movement in the share price. If we think a stock's fair value is $50, and the shares decline to $40 without a change in the intrinsic value of the business, the star rating will go up. Our estimate of what the business is worth hasn't changed, but the shares are more attractive as an investment at $40 than they were at $50.

Shameless Plug: Morningstar.com Premium Members have access to Morningstar Ratings (star ratings) and fair value estimates for nearly 1,600 stocks. Visit Morningstar.com to take a free Premium Membership trial today.

Premium Research

A Different Valuation Approach

Morningstar's fair value estimate analysis is based on a different valuation methodology than ratio-based approaches. If you've ever talked about P/E or P/B (as we did in Lesson 108), you have valued stocks using ratios, also known as multiples. Investors like to use ratios because they are easy to calculate and readily available. The downside is that making sense of valuation ratios usually requires a bit of context. A company can have a high P/E or P/B but still be cheap based on fair value. If a computer company can grow fast enough, its stock will deserve a high P/E, and it might even be a bargain. Likewise, a company in a dying industry with negative growth may have a low P/E and still be overvalued.

We believe that looking at future profits allows for a more sophisticated approach to stock valuation. By determining a company's fair value based on a projection of a company's future cash flows, we can determine whether a stock is undervalued or overvalued. The advantage of this approach is that the result is easy to understand and does not require as much context as the basic ratios. While it takes more time and expertise to estimate future cash flows, we believe that valuing stocks in this way allows investors to spot bargains and make more intelligent investments.

The Bottom Line

Above all, keep in mind that true investing means buying a stake in a superior business at a discounted price and allowing that business to compound in value over a long period of time. It isn't hopping on the latest hot concept hoping for a quick profit. That's why the Morningstar Rating for stocks does not attempt to prognosticate short-term price movements or momentum. We believe that the long-term value of a stock is tied to how much value the company generates for its shareholders.

Morningstar Research Methodology for Valuing Companies

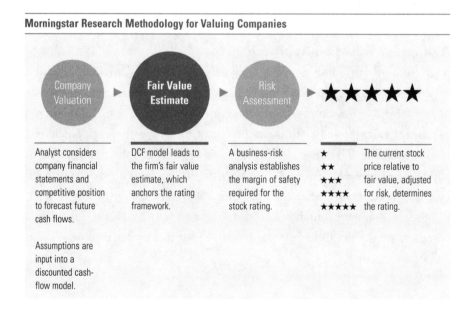

Company Valuation	Fair Value Estimate	Risk Assessment	★★★★★
Analyst considers company financial statements and competitive position to forecast future cash flows. Assumptions are input into a discounted cash-flow model.	DCF model leads to the firm's fair value estimate, which anchors the rating framework.	A business-risk analysis establishes the margin of safety required for the stock rating.	★ ★★ ★★★ ★★★★ ★★★★★ The current stock price relative to fair value, adjusted for risk, determines the rating.

Investor's Checklist

▶ The Morningstar Rating for stocks measures the price of a stock relative to its estimated fair value (adjusted for risk). In other words, it measures whether a stock is overvalued or undervalued relative to its fair value.

▶ The fair value of a stock is the price you would pay today for all the streams of excess cash generated by a company in the future.

▶ Stars are assigned based on the stock's current market price relative to its estimated fair value (adjusted for risk). Stocks trading at larger discounts to their fair values will generally earn higher star ratings. As the quality of a company increases, the discount to fair value required for a 5-star rating decreases.

▶ Fair value estimates do not change very often, but market prices do. As a result, stocks may gain or lose stars based just on the movement in share price.

▶ A fair value estimate is different from looking at valuation ratios such as price/earnings or price/book. A company can have a high P/E or P/B but still be undervalued on a fair value basis.

Quiz

Answers to this quiz can be found on page 172

1   The Morningstar fair value estimate represents which of the following?

a	How much the market expects you to pay for a stock.
b	A stock's current trading price plus its projected earnings growth.
c	An estimate of how much a stock should be worth today based on how much cash flow the company is expected to generate in the future.

2   If a stock has a Morningstar Rating of 3 stars, it is:

a	Overpriced.
b	Cheap.
c	Fairly valued.

3   For which risk level do we require the largest discount (margin of safety) for a stock to become 5 stars?

a	Below-Average.
b	Average.
c	Above-Average.

4   Five-star stocks should generate a return:

a	Greater than the company's cost of equity.
b	Equal to the company's cost of equity.
c	Lower than the company's cost of equity.

5   The Morningstar Rating for stocks:

a	Is based solely on sophisticated computer programs.
b	Is analyst-driven.
c	Takes momentum into account.

Worksheet

1   What is Morningstar's investment philosophy? What is more important: the business underlying a stock or a stock's recent price movements?

Answers to this worksheet can be found on page 183

2   Explain how Morningstar arrives at a fair value and how stars are assigned.

3   Describe the three main ways a stock's star rating can change.

4   How does Morningstar's Rating for stocks differ from other valuation methods?

References

Additional Morningstar Resources

Morningstar isn't just about mutual funds anymore! In addition to this workbook series, Morningstar publishes a number of other products that can help you to become a better, more informed stock investor. These resources can be obtained at your local library, by calling Morningstar directly at 866-608-9570, or by visiting www.morningstar.com.

Morningstar.com

Our Web site features information on stocks, funds, bonds, retirement plans, and much more. In addition to powerful portfolio tools that make tracking investments easier, you'll find daily articles by Morningstar analysts. Much information on the site is free, and there is a reasonably priced Premium Membership service available. Premium Members receive access to more-powerful analytical tools as well as in-depth Analyst Reports (including star ratings and fair value estimates) on nearly 1,600 stocks.

Morningstar® Stocks 500™

Our annual book of full-page reports and unique Morningstar tools helps you uncover the best stock values around. Star ratings, economic moat ratings, fair value estimates, Stewardship Grades, and analyst-written reports make deciding when to buy and sell easy. *Morningstar Stocks 500* makes an excellent desktop reference for throughout the year.

Morningstar® StockInvestor™

StockInvestor is Morningstar's flagship monthly stocks newsletter. Each issue has 32 pages filled with model portfolios, opinions on headline stocks, "red flag" stocks to avoid, and watch lists of wide-moat stocks. To date, both model portfolios in the newsletter (the "Tortoise" and the "Hare") have outperformed the wider stock market, with the "Tortoise" beating it by a large margin.

Morningstar® DividendInvestor™

Interested in generating income from your stock investments? *DividendInvestor* focuses on showing you how to profit from the compound effect of dividends and growth. This monthly newsletter includes a model portfolio and an "On the Bench" watch list of dividend-paying firms worth keeping an eye on.

continued...

Morningstar® Growth Investor™

Now you can be a growth investor while minimizing the normally high risks associated with this style of investing. Our new newsletter helps you spot growth stocks when they can be had at great prices, thus reducing the downside risk. Each issue includes our Growth Portfolio, Growth Giants watch list, companies with Growth at Risk, and more.

The Five Rules for Successful Stock Investing™
Morningstar's Guide to Building Wealth and Winning in the Market

A perfect follow-up to the workbook series, this book, published in 2004, touches on a wide range of stock-related topics, including how to dig into financial statements, how to find great companies that will create shareholder wealth, and how to evaluate companies in all the major sectors. And, of course, it will give you the five rules we think every investor should follow.

Recommended Readings

This workbook series can certainly start you down the path of learning to become a great investor. But as with any intellectual exercise, it pays to both confirm what you've learned as well as to soak up as many other ideas and viewpoints as possible.

Below are what we believe to be some of the most relevant investing books today. These are what we Morningstar analysts have read in forming our own philosophy. We've included classics (*Security Analysis* and *The Intelligent Investor*) as well as those that are more timely and thought-provoking (*Moneyball* and *When Genius Failed*). All are worth reading.

We've tried to group the books since some are light reads easily accessible to new investors, while others require more concentration and experience in order to extract value.

Easy

The Only Investment Guide You'll Ever Need by Andrew Tobias, 2005 (revised). Published by Harvest Books. Maybe not the only guide you'll need, but this is an excellent introduction to investing in general. This book was originally published in 1978 with numerous revisions since then.

Stocks for the Long Run (Third Edition) and *The Future for Investors* by Jeremy J. Siegel, 2002 and 2005, respectively. Published by McGraw-Hill and Crown Business, respectively. Still wondering whether or not to invest in stocks? Professor Siegel's works plainly make the case for equities.

Buffett: The Making of an American Capitalist by Roger Lowenstein, 1996 (Reprint Edition). Published by Main Street Books. One of the many great Warren Buffett books available.

Of Permanent Value: The Story of Warren Buffett by Andrew Kilpatrick, 2005 (revised). Published by Andy Kilpatrick Pub Empire. Yet another excellent book on Warren Buffett and his company, Berkshire Hathaway.

One Up on Wall Street and *Beating the Street* by Peter Lynch, 2000 (Fireside Edition) and 1994, respectively. Published by Simon & Schuster. One of the best investors of his time, Lynch gives insights into how he goes about finding great investments. These are very accessible tomes.

continued...

Why Smart People Make Big Money Mistakes and How to Correct Them: Lessons from the New Science of Behavioral Economics by Gary Belsky and Thomas Gilovich, 2000. Published by Simon & Schuster. This easy read introduces the basics of how psychology and investing interact.

Moneyball by Michael Lewis, 2003. Published by W. W. Norton & Company. What can a book about baseball teach us about investing? This book illustrates how a team tries to find value that no one else sees.

Intermediate

The Essays of Warren Buffett: Lessons for Corporate America by Warren Buffett and Lawrence A. Cunningham, 2001. Published by The Cunningham Group. This book, one of our absolute favorites, contains a collection of Warren Buffett's letters to his shareholders. Buffett's intellect, integrity, and wit shine bright.

The Intelligent Investor: The Definitive Book on Value Investing, Revised Edition by Benjamin Graham and Jason Zweig, 2003. Published by HarperBusiness. The second of Graham's two classics, this book's wisdom still resonates decades after its first publication.

Common Stocks and Uncommon Profits by Philip A. Fisher with Kenneth L. Fisher, 2003 (revised). Published by Wiley. Rather than emphasize cheap stock prices, Fisher focuses on finding great companies that will grow profitably over many years. Buffett's philosophy can be called a marriage between Graham and Fisher. The first edition of this book was published in 1958.

Built to Last by Jim Collins and Jerry Porras, 2002. Published by HarperBusiness. By studying visionary companies, the authors try to find what characteristics great businesses share.

When Genius Failed: The Rise and Fall of Long-Term Capital Management by Roger Lowenstein, 2001. Published by Random House. This book chronicles the spectacular rise and fall of a large trading firm and highlights that no investor can completely beat back risk.

A Random Walk Down Wall Street by Burton G. Malkiel, 2004 (revised). Published by W. W. Norton & Company. This thought-provoking read makes the case for indexing and shows how much of what we attribute as brilliance among money managers may really be random chance.

Value Investing: From Graham to Buffett and Beyond by Bruce Greenwald, Judd Kahn, Paul Sonkin, and Michael van Biema, 2004 (revised). Published by Wiley. This book provides a solid overview of the value-investing philosophy, with profiles of some of the most prominent value investors.

Advanced

Security Analysis: The Classic 1934 Edition by Benjamin Graham and David Dodd, 1934 (republished 1996). Published by McGraw-Hill. This is quite simply the bible of fundamental value investing. It's a true classic, but not light reading.

Financial Statement Analysis: A Practitioner's Guide (Third Edition) by Martin Fridson and Fernando Alvarez, 2002. Published by Wiley. If you want to learn how to dig deeper into a company's financial statements, this is a good guide.

Valuation: Measuring and Managing the Value of Companies (Third Edition) by McKinsey & Company Inc., 2000. Published by Wiley. There are many books on how to value a company, and this is the one that has most often found its way onto Morningstar analysts' shelves.

Competitive Strategy by Michael E. Porter, 1998. Published by Free Press. Want to learn how to think more about competitive advantages and economic moats? This is a must-read.

Triumph of the Optimists: 101 Years of Global Investment Returns by Elroy Dimson, Paul Marsh, and Mike Staunton, 2002. Published by Princeton University Press. This book gives an excellent historical perspective into the long-run returns of a wide variety of investments from around the world.

Industry Web Links

Financial Industry
FDIC (www.fdic.gov)
Mortgage Bankers Association of America (www.mbaa.org)
Financial Research Corporation (www.frcnet.com/frc_home.asp)
National Association of Real Estate Investment Trusts (NAREIT) (www.nareit.com)
National Association of Home Builders (www.nahb.org)
Insurance Journal (www.insurancejournal.com)

Technology Industry
Semiconductor Industry Association (www.sia-online.org/home.cfm)
Glossary of Tech Terms (Whatis.com) (whatis.techtarget.com)
Electronic News (www.reed-electronics.com/electronicnews)
Silicon Strategies (www.siliconstrategies.com)
World Tech News (www.worldtechnews.com)
Computer World (www.computerworld.com)

Heavy Industry
Department of Transportation (www.dot.gov)
Bureau of Transportation Statistics (www.bts.gov)
Federal Railroad Administration (www.fra.dot.gov)
American Trucking Associations (www.truckline.com)
Steel Glossary (American Iron and Steel Institute)
    (www.steel.org/learning/glossary/glossary.htm)
Aluminum Association (www.aluminum.org)
American Iron and Steel Institute (www.steel.org)
Aerospace Industries Association (www.aia-aerospace.org)
Defense News (www.defensenews.com)

Natural-Resources Industry
Random Lengths (www.randomlengths.com)
The World of Gold (www.gold.org)
The Silver Institute (www.silverinstitute.org)
Mining Media (www.mining-media.com/ca/index.aspx)
How Stuff Works (science.howstuffworks.com)
Platinum Today (www.platinum.matthey.com)

Consumer and Retail Industry

International Council of Shopping Centers (www.icsc.org)

Shopper Trak (www.shoppertrak.com/news.html)

DSN Retailing Today (www.dsnretailingtoday.com)

Beverage World (www.beverageworld.com)

Baking Business (www.bakingbusiness.com)

Health-Care Industry

Clinical Trials (www.clinicaltrials.gov)

FDA (www.fda.gov)

Pharmaceutical Executive (www.pharmexec.com/pharmexec)

Centers for Medicare and Medicaid Services (www.cms.hhs.gov)

Biotech Industry Organization (www.bio.org)

BioWorld (www.bioworld.com)

Center Watch (www.centerwatch.com)

Energy and Utilities Industry

Energy Information Administration (www.eia.doe.gov)

Rigzone (www.rigzone.com)

Oil & Gas Journal (ogj.pennnet.com/home.cfm)

Federal Energy Regulatory Commission (www.ferc.gov)

Bureau of Land Management (www.blm.gov)

Pipeline 101 (www.pipeline101.com/index.html)

OPEC (www.opec.org)

Hotels and Entertainment Industry

Hotel & Motel (www.hotelmotel.com/hotelmotel)

Smith Travel Research (www.smithtravelresearch.com)

Travel Industry Association of America (http://www.tia.org/Travel/default.asp)

Quiz 101: Stocks Versus Other Investments

1 a. Of the types of investments listed, stocks provide the largest long-term returns. In attempting to reach your financial goals in life, maximizing the return on your investment dollars is key.

2 a. Stocks are the most volatile. Over the long term, stocks have a higher return than bonds or savings accounts. But this volatility means that over the short term, other types of investments may significantly outperform stocks.

3 c. Understanding advanced statistics is not needed to be a successful stock investor. The vast majority of people have all the basic skills required.

4 c. Savings accounts provide the lowest real (or inflation-adjusted) return over the long term.

5 b. When you buy a stock, you are buying an ownership interest in a company. Bonds are loans from companies and the government.

Quiz 102: The Magic of Compounding

1 b. 72 divided by 10% equals about 7.

2 c. The money would double every six years (72/12). Therefore you'd have $20,000 after the first six years, and $40,000 after 12 years.

3 c. A financial calculator is not a component of compound interest. The three factors are time, the rate of return, and the amount of money invested.

4 c. $1,000,000 divided by 2 equals $500,000. Remember, it is the last few years of compound interest that have the largest absolute impact.

5 b. The higher the interest rate, the more money you'll have in the future.

Quiz 103: Investing for the Long Run

1   a.   The average yearly difference between the high and low of a typical stock is between 30% and 50%. In other words, over the short term, a stock can be quite volatile.

2   c.   You should purchase stocks only if you are investing for more than five years.

3   b.   Stocks have returned more than bonds and cash after any 10-year period. This has held true even if you had the misfortune of investing at only the market peaks.

4   c.   Just because a stock is well-known does not mean it's a good investment. General Motors has actually underperformed the stock market for the last 40 years.

5   c.   Over the long run, stocks have had a higher return than bonds, but their returns are not guaranteed. You should invest in stocks only for goals that are five years or more away.

Quiz 104: What Matters and What Doesn't

1   c.   The more frequently you trade, the higher your tax bill. This is because capital gains will be realized more often. (See Chapter 9 for more on taxes.) Trading activity is actually inversely correlated to returns. The more you trade, the more commissions you will incur.

2   a.   "Mr. Market" tends to be temperamental, over-reacting to near-term news. If the market were perfectly efficient and correctly valued future cash flows at all times, stock prices would not be so volatile.

3   b.   The future profits a company can generate will drive the price of its stock over the long term. Over the short term, any number of factors may influence a company's stock price.

4   c.   Remember that successful stock investing is like chess, where thought, patience, and the ability to peer into the future are rewarded. Stock investing is not about trading.

5   b.   You should pay the most attention to a company's competitive positioning, which in turn will determine future profits. In our opinion, broader stock market predictions as well as those based on stock price charts are of nearly zero value.

Quiz 105: The Purpose of a Company

1   b.   A stock is an ownership interest in a company. Although companies receive money from stock offerings, it is more important to remember that a stock represents a stake in a company. Stocks should not be considered vehicles for speculative trading.

2   c.   The purpose of a company is to take money from investors and generate profits on their investments. Companies do not guarantee that they will make investors rich quickly. Although bad management teams spend money on lavish corporate expenses, that shouldn't be the purpose of a company.

3   a.   If the company goes bankrupt, bondholders get paid before stockholders. Remember that stockholders are the "residual" claimants of a company's profits, which means they get paid after everybody else. If a company goes bankrupt, they get what's left over after all the creditors are paid. Bonds typically do not yield higher returns than stocks when a company does well. The government doesn't pay a company's interest on a corporate bond if the company can't pay for it—the company is responsible for the interest payment.

4   b.   Company B is more profitable. Although Company A generates profits of $500 million, which is greater in absolute terms than Company B's $250 million in profits, Company A has a lower return on capital. For every $1 that investors put into Company A, they get back $0.10 in profits per year. However, for every $1 that investors put into Company B, they get back $0.20 per year.

5   b.   As a company adds shares outstanding, your ownership interest in the firm decreases. Shareholders can benefit more from owning one share of a billion-dollar company that has only 100 shares (a 1% ownership interest) than by owning 100 shares of a billion-dollar company that has a million shares outstanding (a 0.01% ownership interest).

Quiz 106: Gathering Relevant Information

1   c.   A company's 10-K is a must-read annual report filed with the SEC. It is the most comprehensive of the public filings and contains audited financial statements.

2   a.   A company's 10-Q is a quarterly report filed with the SEC. It contains unaudited financial statements.

3   b.   The form 4 contains information about stock trading made by company insiders.

4   b.   Financial statements are audited by an external accounting firm in the 10-K. The financial statements in the 10-Q are generally not audited.

5   c.   Independent analyst research reports sometimes provide a different perspective compared with information published by the company itself.

Quiz 107: Introduction to Financial Statements

1   b.   A company's profits are the difference between how much it brought in (its revenues) and how much it spent (its expenses) during a given period.

2   c.   The statement of cash flows has three sections: cash flows from operating activities, cash flows from investing activities, and cash flows from financing activities.

3   c.   A company with lots of assets relative to liabilities would have relatively high equity (Assets − Liabilities = Equity) and less risk of going bankrupt. Generally speaking, companies with lots of assets relative to liabilities are healthier and more resistant to setbacks than companies with lots of liabilities.

4   a.   Current assets are likely to be used up or converted into cash within one business cycle, usually defined as one year.

5   b.   The statement of cash flows excludes noncash revenues and expenses, showing actual cash flows. Both the income statement and statement of cash flows show results for a period of time like a quarter or a year, and the income statement—not the statement of cash flows—provides a breakdown of revenues, expenses, and profits.

Quiz 108: Learn the Lingo—Basic Ratios

1   c.   The P/E is determined by dividing the price per share ($30) by the earnings per share ($1.50), yielding a P/E of 20 in this case.

2   b.   The earnings yield is calculated by inverting the P/E ratio. In this case the earnings yield is 1/30 or 3.3%.

3   a.   Company A is generating more earnings per dollar of sales than Company B. This means Company A needs fewer sales to generate the same level of earnings, and the market is likely to reward Company A with a higher P/S ratio.

4   a.   A rising dividend yield means that the stock is becoming less expensive because a higher percentage of the stock price is being paid out in annual dividends.

5   c.   For a company with negative accounting earnings, it is possible to use either the price/sales ratio or price/cash flow ratio.

Quiz 109: Stocks and Taxes

1   a.   The lowered tax rates will expire in 2009, unless they are extended.

2   c.   A Roth IRA offers tax-free distributions, as long as certain rules are met. The downside is that Roth IRAs must be funded with after-tax dollars.

3   b.   You would prefer to own in a taxable account the stock in a solid business that grows steadily over time, but pays no dividends. This would allow you to hold the stock for a long time, deferring the realization of capital gains. Dividends would be taxable.

4   a.   You must generally begin making mandatory withdrawals from 401(k) and traditional IRA accounts when you reach 70 1/2.

5   a.   Your five-taxable-year period for Roth IRAs starts on Jan. 1 of the tax year when you make your first contribution or conversion into a Roth IRA.

Quiz 110: Using Financial Services Wisely

1   c.   It will cost $10,000 to purchase 100 shares at $100. Since you are buying on margin, and borrow 50% of the funds, you put up only $5,000. The stock goes up 10%, so the value of the 100 shares is now $11,000, a $1,000 increase. The return on your investment, however, is 20% ($1,000/$5,000).

2   b.   Think of a broker as the middleman between you and the person you are buying your stock from or selling your stock to. When you place an order to either buy or sell a stock, your broker will find a party that is willing to take the other side of your transaction.

3   c.   You'll borrow 100 shares and immediately sell them to receive $2,000 (100 shares x $20/share). Once the stock drops to $15, you buy the shares back for $1,500. Your cash profit is $500 (cash received of $2,000 minus cash paid of $1,500).

4   a.   A market order tells the broker to buy or sell at the best price available, and the trades are usually executed immediately, assuming the market is open.

5   b.   Though full-service brokers certainly charge large commissions, they do provide personal attention and advice, and they deserve to get paid for it. An inherent problem with paying for advice via commissions is that the advisor gets paid more the more you trade, and trading frequently is typically not in your best interests.

Quiz 111: Understanding the News

1   b.   The divisor used to calculate the Dow has been shrinking steadily in recent years to account for arbitrary events such as stock splits and changes in the composition of the roster.

2   a.   Microsoft is the only company out of the three choices that is a member of the S&P 500. Berkshire Hathaway is excluded because it primarily holds stock of other companies. Royal Dutch Petroleum is not a member of the S&P 500 because it is not a U.S. company.

3   a.   The Dow is price-weighted. The Nasdaq Composite Index and the S&P 500 Index are market-cap-weighted.

continued…

4   b.   An "earnings surprise" happens when a company's actual earnings results are different than what Wall Street's analysts expect. A stock split is when a company issues more shares to its shareholders, and the stock price falls to account for the ownership dilution.

5   c.   A slight earnings miss or analyst downgrade would not explicitly change a company's intrinsic value, and both events are very short-term focused. An SEC investigation into accounting could materially impact the investment outlook, however.

Quiz 112: Start Thinking Like an Analyst

1   a.   Many restaurants are quite profitable, and not all of them spend money on branding. Still, there is a lot of competition in the industry, and it's very easy to walk across the street to a rival restaurant, so the switching costs are very low.

2   a.   Economic moats allow a company to generate profits and keep competitors at bay. Companies that reward investors over the long haul are those that have a durable competitive advantage.

3   c.   High switching costs help companies raise prices without the risk of losing customers. If it's costly for a firm's customers to switch products, either in terms of money, time, or convenience, then the company is better positioned to pass along price increases.

4   b.   Technological expertise is not a type of economic moat. Technological expertise can form the foundation for an economic moat, but it is rare that the expertise provides a sustainable, long-term competitive advantage, because improvements in technology are often easily imitated.

5   b.   eBay is the quintessential example of a company with a strong network effect.

Quiz 113: Investing for the Long Term

1 c. Morningstar's fair value estimate represents how much a stock should be worth today based on how much cash flow the company is expected to generate in the future. The Morningstar fair value estimate should not be confused with a target price, which is how much the market might be willing to pay for a stock. To arrive at a fair value, Morningstar analysts use a detailed discounted cash-flow model that factors in projections for the company's income statement, balance sheet, and cash-flow statement. It is not adding projected earnings growth to a stock's current trading price.

2 c. Stocks that are trading very close to our analysts' fair value estimates will usually get 3-star ratings. Assuming that the stock's market price and fair value eventually converge, 3-star stocks should offer a "fair return." A fair return is one that adequately compensates you for the riskiness of the stock.

3 c. We require the largest margin of safety for the riskiest stocks before they can become 5 stars. Companies with below-average risk require modest discounts to our fair value estimate in order to become 5 stars.

4 a. Five-star stocks should offer investors a return that is greater than the company's cost of equity. The cost of equity is often called the "required return," because it represents the return an investor requires for taking on the risk of owning a stock. Since 5-star stocks are considerably undervalued, we expect investors will enjoy high returns that significantly exceed the risks associated with investing in the stock.

5 b. The Morningstar Rating is analyst-driven. At Morningstar, we estimate a company's fair value by determining how much we would pay today for all the streams of excess cash generated by the company in the future. We arrive at this value by forecasting a company's future financial performance using a detailed discounted cash-flow model that factors in projections for the company's income statement, balance sheet, and cash-flow statement. The result is an analyst-driven estimate of the stock's fair value.

Worksheet 101: Stocks Versus Other Investments

1   Whatever your long-term financial goals may be, stock investing can help you reach them. The payoffs certainly justify the effort required to learn how to invest in stocks.

2   Stocks may indeed be the most volatile investment class, but they also offer the highest long-term return. As long as you are prepared for and expect the volatility ahead of time, it can make the periodic dips a lot less scary.

3   Stocks are ownership interests in companies, not just pieces of paper to be traded.

4   Remember, stocks are ownership interests in businesses, and chances are you can become an owner in the companies that you have listed. But do keep in mind that just because you like a company's product does not mean that company is a good investment. This workbook series will help you sort it all out.

Worksheet 102: The Magic of Compounding

1   Here is an example:

Age	Investment Value ($)
30	30,000
36	60,000
42	120,000
48	240,000
54	480,000
60	960,000
66	1,920,000
72	3,840,000
78	7,680,000
84	15,360,000
90	30,720,000

Again, are you surprised? Why isn't everyone a millionaire?

continued…

2   There are scores of ways one could accumulate a million dollars. In our example, Luke became a millionaire by investing $2,000 per year for six years beginning at age 24 and earning 12% until age 65. Given the time horizon to your financial goals, are you investing enough to reach those goals?

3   You can control or at least influence all three of the components of compound interest: the amount invested, your rate of return, and the time you allow the investments to work for you. Remember, the earlier you start and the more you put in, the greater the payoff. You can influence your rate of return by studying to become an educated investor.

Worksheet 103: Investing for the Long Run

1   Assuming you will buy a car sometime in the next couple of years, you should most certainly not invest the funds earmarked for your car in the stock market. Investing in stocks for such short-term goals can expose you to significant risk. Stocks tend to be quite volatile in the short term, and you could be forced to sell at exactly the wrong time if you happened to need that new car during a market dip. The further away your financial goal, the more sense it makes to invest in stocks.

2   Since Janet's financial goals are so far in the future, it makes perfect sense for her to put all of her investment money in stocks. Starting investing early can give one a giant leg up later in life.

3   When investing in stocks to meet your financial goals, make sure these goals are far enough out in the future to minimize the risk of short-term volatility wiping out your returns. It's also worth restating that stocks are volatile investments and being prepared for this volatility can reduce the likelihood of being tempted to sell at the wrong times.

4   Those who started investing in the late 1990s and expected to see their portfolios grow by 50% or more annually learned a difficult lesson in the recent bear market. Don't let unrealistic expectations ruin your investing experience. If you wrote down anything greater than 15% for the 10-year return, you are probably going to be disappointed. A return of 9%-12% is probably closer to what you should expect your stock investments to achieve.

Worksheet 104: What Matters and What Doesn't

1   One does not need speedy reflexes, a fancy suit, and fast computers to be a successful investor. Patience, an understanding of how companies work, and the ability to perceive future trends are far more important characteristics to have.

2   Active traders have three things working against them: the bid/ask spread, commissions, and taxes. The less often you trade, the less often you will incur these costs.

3   You will likely come across a frightening number of ridiculous investing approaches being promoted. Before partaking in any investing approach (including those put forward by Morningstar), ask yourself, "Does this make intellectual sense?"

4   Your guess is as good as any. Perhaps you will be lucky and be right, but probably not. It's amazing how often experts get asked this question, and how few of those predictions actually pan out. Remember, you buy stocks, not the market.

Worksheet 105: The Purpose of a Company

1   **Advantages:**   ▶ You are a part owner of the company.
    ▶ You are entitled to vote on important company matters.
    ▶ You stand to benefit the most when the company does well. This includes dividend payments the company may make to its shareholders.

   Disadvantages: ▶ You are the last claimant of the company's profits.
   ▶ You do not get a fixed return on your investment.
   ▶ You stand to lose the most when the company does poorly.

2   Debt capital and equity capital present investors with different return opportunities because they each have different risk profiles. Creditors supplying companies with debt capital shoulder less risk, so their return is typically lower and fixed. On the other hand, shareholders supplying companies with equity capital bear all the risks of ownership. Their return is directly tied to the company's underlying business performance. When a company earns lots of profits, shareholders stand to benefit the most.

continued…

3   Return on capital is the ratio of profit to capital invested. It is a measure of a company's underlying profitability. Return on stock is the sum of capital gains (stock appreciation) and dividends. Unlike return on capital, return on stock reflects the investing public's opinion about the company's present and future performance, which are subjective measures. Over the long term, underlying business performance and return on capital will drive share prices.

4   Return on capital and return on stock will ultimately converge in the long run. Therefore, a high return on capital that is sustainable over a long period of time will yield a high return on stock. Conversely, keep in mind that a high return on stock may not be sustainable if return on capital is low.

Worksheet 106: Gathering Relevant Information

1   The 10-K can be some dense reading, but it also provides a wealth of information about a company. After reading it, you should come away with a better sense of where a company's businesses are heading, as well as some of the risks they are facing. How well is a company's existing service performing? Is a new product on the horizon? How healthy are the relationships with employees? Is there a major lawsuit hanging over the firm? You would be much better prepared to answer these questions after reading a company's 10-K.

2   Before buying any stock, it is imperative that you read the public filings to gain an understanding of exactly what kind of business you are investing in. Creating watch lists will certainly help you to track a large number of potential investments, as well as stay in the loop on the ones you already own.

3   Proxy statements are perhaps the most helpful of the public filings for assessing the quality and trustworthiness of a company's management. For the company you chose, you should be able to locate the CEO's salary and how many shares of the company he or she owns.

4   While companies are required by law to tell the truth about their businesses, they often only tell part of the story. When considering any potential investment, it's important to try to view the pros and cons from several different perspectives. You can often get this perspective from industry Web sites, newspapers, magazines, and letters from mutual fund managers.

Worksheet 107: Introduction to Financial Statements

1   The income statement tells you how much money a company has brought in (its revenues), how much it has spent (its expenses), and the difference between the two (its profit). The income statement shows a company's revenues and expenses over a specific time frame such as three months or a year. The balance sheet basically tells you how much a company owns (its assets) and how much it owes (its liabilities) at a given point in time. The difference between what it owns and what it owes is its equity. The statement of cash flows tells you how much cash went into and out of a company during a specific time frame like a quarter or a year.

2   If…Assets = Equity + Liabilities
    Then…Liabilities = Assets – Equity.

    For this problem, liabilities = $110 million – $60 million. Or, $50 million.

3   Gross profit is calculated as revenues minus cost of goods sold. Operating profit is gross profit minus overhead operating expenses, namely SG&A. Net income is operating income minus all interest, tax and other expenses.

4   The statement of cash flows is needed due to the concept of accrual accounting. There is often a difference between when a firm accounts for its revenues and expenses and when the cash actually comes in and leaves the company.

Worksheet 108: Learn the Lingo—Basic Ratios

1   The quick and dirty ways to value a company include using the P/E ratio, the earnings yield, the PEG ratio, the P/S ratio, the P/B ratio, the P/CF ratio, and the dividend yield.

2   Cash flow can be less subject to accounting manipulation than earnings because it measures actual cash. Accrual accounting can also give a company that is bleeding cash positive earnings. Moreover, it can cause companies with robust cash flow to report negative earnings.

    continued…

3	Stock Price?	$50	($500M/10M = $50)
	EPS?	$2.50	($25M/10M = $2.50)
	P/E?	20	($50/$2.50 = 20)
	Earnings Yield?	5%	(1/20 = 5%)

4	Market Capitalization?	$20B	($20 x 1B = $20 B)
	Book Value Per Share?	$10	($10B/1B = $10)
	P/B?	2	($20/$10 = 2)
	Dividend Yield?	5.0%	($1/$20 = 5.0%)

Worksheet 109: Stocks and Taxes

1   Answer: $50.

Your cost basis for your Microsoft shares is $3,000 (100 shares x $30) and your sale netted $4,000. Therefore, your capital gain is $1,000. Since you are in the 15% income tax bracket, you qualify for the 5% capital gains tax rate. On your $1,000 gain, you owe $50 ($1,000 x 5%) of capital gains tax.

Your cost basis for your Intel shares is $5,000 (200 shares x $25) and your sale netted $10,000. Your capital gain is $5,000. Since you are in the 15% income tax bracket, you qualify for the 5% capital gains tax rate. Furthermore, in 2008, the 5% rate drops to 0%. You owe no taxes on your $5,000 capital gain.

2   The main tax-advantaged accounts available to investors are 401(k) accounts, traditional IRAs, and Roth IRAs.

3   You could realize the gains and losses at the same time so that they offset. This would result in only $5,000 of the $15,000 capital gain being taxable. Another option would be to defer all the unrealized capital gains further while realizing $3,000 of the capital losses per year. This is because up to $3,000 of capital losses can be used to offset ordinary income after capital gains, if any, are offset.

Worksheet 110: Using Financial Services Wisely

1   Discount brokers provide bare-bones service at a very inexpensive cost. Meanwhile, full-service brokers will provide a much wider range of services, commonly including investment research and personalized advice. These services typically come at a high cost, however.

2   Shorting stocks could be risky because the potential for loss is unlimited. You could very easily lose many times more than what you could have gained from a single trading position if a stock you short increases in value.

3   A market order tells the broker to buy or sell at the best price he or she can get in the market, and the trade is usually executed immediately. A limit order allows you to set the maximum price you are willing to pay for a stock, or a minimum price you'd be willing to sell a stock for. Because you are placing limitations on your order, it may not be executed immediately.

4   Costs, the level of customer service, and peripheral services offered are some of the things to consider before choosing a discount broker.

Worksheet 111: Understanding the News

1   Answer: $1 / 0.125 = 8$ points.

   Part 2: $-\$1 / 0.125 = -8$ points
            $-\$1 / 0.125 = -8$ points
            $-\$5 / 0.125 = -40$ points
            Total -56 points

2   Some people trade on every little piece of news. Others may think a bump in the road is the edge of a cliff.

   It's important to remember that Wall Street tends to be very shortsighted, since it is driven by short-term performance goals. (Analysts and fund managers are often slaves to the "What have you done for me lately?" mentality.) This provides those with a long-term view the luxury of not worrying about most of this short-term noise.

continued...

3   Below are some examples of news, though there are certainly more. There is also a lot of gray area here, but with experience you will better understand what is the tip of an iceberg versus a simple ice cube.

Noise (i.e., things that do not impact future cash flow):
Wall Street analyst upgrade/downgrade
Earnings surprise
Former company CEO in sex scandal
Famous investor mentions company in business press

Meaningful (i.e., things that impact future cash flow):
SEC investigation into accounting
Lawsuit loss
Operations significantly impacted by natural disaster
Product recall

Worksheet 112: Start Thinking Like an Analyst

1   There is no correct answer for this exercise. Just remember the framework that can help get you started thinking like an analyst:

1. What is the goal of the business?
2. How does the business make money?
3. How well is the business actually doing?
4. How well is the business positioned relative to its competitors?

2   The four types of economic moats are:
Low-cost producer
High switching costs
Network effect
Intangible assets

3   Adobe Systems, maker of Adobe Acrobat and Photoshop, is a wide-moat company with a network effect moat (and that's not the only moat it has, by the way). Its easily downloadable software has become the standard for reading and creating documents electronically. Some other examples include Microsoft with its Windows operating system for computers and American Express with its credit card system.

continued...

4   Determining economic moats helps investors separate great companies from those that are merely good. It also helps identify those firms that have the sustainable, long-term competitive advantage necessary to generate above-average profits for a long period of time.

Worksheet 113: Investing for the Long Term

1   At Morningstar, we evaluate stocks as pieces of a business and not as "little wiggling things with charts attached." We believe that purchasing shares of superior businesses at discounts to their fair values, and allowing those businesses to compound value over long periods of time, is the surest way to create wealth in the stock market. We believe that watching minute-by-minute stock trades is a largely fruitless exercise.

2   At Morningstar, we arrive at a fair value by forecasting a company's future financial performance using a detailed discounted cash-flow model that factors in five-year projections for the company's income statement, balance sheet, and cash-flow statement. Morningstar assigns stars based on the stock's market price relative to its estimated fair value, adjusted for risk. Generally speaking, stocks trading at large discounts to our analysts' fair value estimates will receive higher (4 or 5) star ratings, and stocks trading at large premiums to their fair value estimates will receive lower (1 or 2) star ratings. Stocks that are trading very close to our analysts' fair value estimates will usually get 3-star ratings.

3   Stock star ratings are updated daily, and therefore they can change daily. The ratings can change because of a move in the stock's price, a change in the analyst's estimate of the stock's fair value, a change in the analyst's assessment of a company's business risk, or a combination of any of these factors.

4   Morningstar's fair value estimate analysis is based on a different valuation methodology than ratio-based approaches. We believe that looking at future profits allows for a more sophisticated approach to stock valuation. By determining a company's fair value based on a projection of the company's future cash flows, we can determine whether a stock is undervalued or overvalued. The advantage of this approach is that the result is easy to understand and does not require as much context as valuation ratios. While it takes more time and expertise to estimate future cash flows, we believe that valuing stocks in this way allows investors to spot bargains and make more intelligent investments.

Investing Terms

10-K

The statutory annual report of a company's activities that is filed with the Securities and Exchange Commission. The 10-K tends to be the most comprehensive of a company's periodic filings. Note that these reports contain audited financial statements, whereas the statements within quarterly reports (10-Qs) are not audited.

10-Q

The statutory quarterly report of a company's activities that is filed with the Securities and Exchange Commission. The 10-Q tends to be less comprehensive than the annual (10-K) filing but provides useful short-term information and changes within the company. Note that the financial statements contained in a quarterly report are unaudited, unlike those in annual (10-K) reports.

20-F

Annual report submitted to the Securities and Exchange Commission by foreign companies that are publicly traded on a U.S. exchange. The 20-F is similar to the 10-K submitted by U.S. companies.

401(k)

A regulated defined-contribution retirement account set up by companies for their employees. The name comes from the IRS code that governs the plans.

Participants in 401(k)s are allowed to direct a portion of their pretax income into accounts that are allowed to grow tax-free. Distributions are taxed (at a presumably lower tax rate in retirement), and early distributions before retirement age are generally penalized.

40-F

The annual report filed with the Securities and Exchange Commission by Canadian companies that are publicly traded on a U.S. exchange. The 40-F is similar to the 10-K report that U.S. companies must file.

A

Accounts Payable

An accounting entry on the liabilities side of the balance sheet that typically represents what companies owe to their vendors.

Accounts Receivable

An accounting entry on the asset side of the balance sheet that typically represents bills outstanding for services already rendered. One company's accounts receivable is usually another company's accounts payable.

Accrual Accounting

A method of accounting in which revenue is recorded when earned and expenses are recorded when incurred. This recognition of earnings and expenses may not correspond to when cash is actually received or spent. Publicly traded companies in the United States use accrual accounting.

American Depository Receipt (ADR)

A certificate issued by a bank that represents a set number of shares in a foreign corporation. ADRs make it easier for Americans to invest in foreign companies. They are traded on an exchange like stocks, which allows for liquidity and current price information.

American Stock Exchange (AMEX)

One of a number of U.S. stock exchanges where investors can trade shares of certain companies.

Amortization

1. The gradual, systematic elimination of a liability.

2. A noncash expense that represents the decline of an intangible asset's value over time.

Analyst Upgrades/Downgrades

A revision in a Wall Street analyst's rating, such as "Buy," "Hold," or "Sell," for a particular stock. When a stock's rating is upgraded or downgraded, the stock price will often move in that direction.

Anchoring

A behavioral finance term used to describe investors' tendency to place undue emphasis on recent performance or an irrelevant data point, such as the purchase price of a stock.

Annual Report

A report provided by a company to its shareholders that includes information on the company's activities in the past fiscal year. The term "annual report" may refer to the 10-K filed with the SEC or the less comprehensive glossy report distributed by a company that may have only a portion of the information contained in the 10-K.

Annual Shareholder Meeting

The annual gathering of shareholders of public firms to review new company developments and vote on any outstanding matters.

Annuity

A financial instrument that makes fixed payments over a predetermined number of periods.

Asset

Any item that a company may own. Assets include cash, property, buildings, machinery, and so on.

Asset Class

A category of investments with similar characteristics. Some of the most common asset classes include stocks, bonds, mutual funds, real estate, bank accounts, and cash.

Asset/Equity Ratio

Total assets divided by total shareholders' equity. The asset/equity ratio (also known as the equity multiplier) is indicative of a company's liquidity and stability. Generally, a high asset/equity ratio is worthy of concern but should be viewed within the context of a company's industry peers.

Asset Turnover Ratio

A measure of how many dollars in revenue a company has generated per each dollar of assets, calculated as sales divided by total assets. Generally, the higher this ratio, the more efficient the company.

B

Baby Put

A put option that is far out of the money with a subsequently small price.

Balance Sheet

A financial statement that shows what a company owns (its assets), what it owes (its liabilities), and the difference between the two (its equity). The balance sheet, one of the three main financial statements, is a snapshot of a company's financial health at a specific point in time such as the end of the year.

Barrier to Entry

A hypothetical obstruction to competition such as brand strength, economies of scale, patents, and copyrights that protect the profits of a company. *See Economic Moat.*

Basic Shares

The number of shares of stock that a company has outstanding. This is often compared with the diluted share count, which accounts for the effects of shares that could be issued via options and convertible bonds.

Basis

The purchase price of a capital asset such as stocks or bonds. Basis (also known as cost basis) is important in computing potential capital gains taxes.

Behavioral Finance

The study of how human psychology affects financial decision-making.

Beta

A statistical measure of the volatility of a given stock relative to the volatility of the overall market. *See Volatility.*

Bid/Ask Spread

The difference between the highest price someone in the market is willing to pay for a stock (the bidding price) and the lowest price for which someone is willing to sell a stock (the asking price). In general, the larger the market for a given stock, the lower the spread will be. The bid/ask spread is one of the frictional costs of trading.

Board of Directors

A collection of individuals elected by shareholders to steer a company in the most profitable direction. In most situations, company executives (CEO, CFO, etc.) report to the board of directors. Executives are hired, fired, and directed by their boards, not shareholders directly.

Bond

A loan made to a company or government for a certain amount of time (the bond's term or maturity) typically in return for regular interest payments, otherwise known as coupons. Bonds are the primary way companies raise debt capital to finance their operations.

Book Value

1. The value of an asset on the balance sheet calculated as historical cost less accumulated depreciation.

2. The theoretical value of a company if it were immediately liquidated today, calculated as total assets minus liabilities, intangible assets, and preferred stock. Book value is represented on the balance sheet as common equity. Value investors often start their research for undervalued companies with those that are trading at or below their book value.

Buffett, Warren

Chairman and CEO of Berkshire Hathaway and renowned value investor. Also known as the "Oracle of Omaha," Warren Buffett is considered by some to be the greatest investor of our generation and by others to be the greatest investor of all time. He is most often associated with value investing, where intrinsic value is paramount. Buffett's stellar investing record is often used to show that the market is not perfectly efficient and that high-level statistics are not necessary to become an outstanding investor.

Buyer Power

The negotiating strength of a product's purchaser. Strong buyers put pressure on sellers to decrease prices while maintaining or increasing quality. Buyer power is an important component to Michael Porter's Five Forces Model.

Bylaws

Rules governing management established by a company when incorporated.

C

Call

An option represented by a contract that allows the purchaser to buy a stock from a second party at a given price within a certain amount of time. The other party, or "writer of the call," is obligated to provide the stock and is compensated for this risk by a premium—the price of the contract. The call holder will exercise the option only when the strike price of the call is less than the current market price. The difference between these two numbers, less the premium paid, is the call holder's gain.

Capital

The cash or other resources that a company uses to make money. Generally, a company tries to achieve the greatest income with as little capital as possible. There are two types of capital—debt capital (provided by lenders) and equity capital (provided by owners). When a company sells stock in itself, it is raising equity capital.

Capital Asset Pricing Model (CAPM)

An efficient market theory convention that calculates the value of a stock as the risk-free rate plus that stock's beta (*see Volatility*) times the market premium.

Capital Gain/Loss

Gain or loss realized when an asset, such as a stock or bond, is sold for more or less than its basis, or original purchase price.

Cash Accounting

Method of accounting in which revenue is recorded when cash is received, and expenses are recorded when cash is spent. This can be contrasted with accrual accounting.

Cash Flow Statement

See Statement of Cash Flows.

Cash Flow to the Firm

One of the methods of valuing a company via a discounted cash-flow analysis. This measures cash flow independent of the capital structure.

Charter

A filing that describes the basic purposes of a proposed company. The charter is also known as the articles of incorporation.

Circle of Competence

The area of one's investing aptitude. Investors often fare best when they stay within their circle of competence when selecting investments—in other words, "stick to what you know."

Cognitive Dissonance

A psychological term used to describe the inability to hold two seemingly disparate ideas, opinions, beliefs, attitudes, or behaviors at once.

Commissions

The fees paid to brokers and financial advisors for the services they provide, including executing trades. Any profit-maximizing investor should seek to minimize commissions paid.

Compensation Committee

A group usually composed of company insiders and board members that determines appropriate executive incentives, which generally consist of salary, bonuses, and stock options.

Competitive Position

The ability of one company to outperform another company based on a variety of attributes. *See Economic Moat.*

Compound Interest

Interest that accrues on top of interest, or gains that beget more gains. To calculate the future value of an investment, you need to know the investment amount, the rate of return (or interest rate), and the number of periods the investment will be allowed to compound.

Confirmation Bias

A psychological term describing how people treat information that supports what is already believed, or desired, more favorably.

Contract

An agreement between the writer and the buyer of an option to either buy or sell a stock at a given price. This agreement gives the purchaser the "option" to purchase (or sell) the security, while requiring the writer of the contract to sell (or buy) if the option holder so chooses.

Corporate Governance

Internal and external controls that promote and maintain fair business practices. *See Stewardship.*

Cost of Capital

The expenses a company incurs from the use of debt or equity, usually expressed as a percentage. The weighted average cost of capital combines the cost of equity and the cost of debt into a single rate used to discount cash flows when valuing a company using the cash flow to the firm method.

Cost of Debt

The return investors in a company's debt receive in exchange for taking on risk. The cost of debt is determined by the credit quality of a firm. The riskier the firm, the higher its cost of debt.

Cost of Equity

The return equity investors expect to receive on their investment for the risk they are assuming when becoming an owner. A company's cost of equity is less tangible than its cost of debt. In general, a riskier company will have a higher cost of equity.

Cost of Goods Sold (COGS)

Expenses, such as for raw materials or labor, found on the income statement that are directly related to the goods or services provided by a company. For many companies, COGS (also known as "cost of sales") is the largest expense incurred and is therefore important in determining profitability.

Creditor

The person or institution, such as a bank, that loans money to a borrower in exchange for interest and the eventual return of principal. Creditors provide debt capital to companies.

Cyclicals

The stocks of companies whose prosperity tends to be heavily dependent on economic growth. Cyclicals tend to be capital-intensive businesses, such as auto and steel makers, that perform extremely well when economic growth is strong, but struggle, sometimes severely, when growth is weak or recessionary.

D

Day Trading

The act of quickly trading in and out of stocks in an often futile attempt to accumulate a large quantity of small gains caused by intraday fluctuations in stock prices. Those who trade excessively work against the tide in terms of both taxes and commissions.

Deferred Revenue

An accounting liability created by accrual accounting when a company collects cash ahead of when it recognizes revenue. The cash is already in the door, but the liability is the promise of future goods or services.

Degree of Rivalry

A component of Michael Porter's Five Forces Model that indicates the intensity of competition in an industry. The higher the degree of rivalry, the more difficult it is for firms to raise prices and maintain profitability.

Depreciation

A noncash expense that represents an asset's normal wear and tear. Depreciation reduces the book value of the asset.

Deworsifiers

Peter Lynch's parody of diversifiers. Lynch argues that investors or companies who overstressed the importance of diversification often "deworsified" their performance by diluting their good ideas just to achieve variety.

Diluted Shares

The total number of shares a company would have outstanding if all potentially convertible securities, such as options or convertible bonds, were converted into shares (i.e., basic shares plus converted shares).

Discount Factor

In a discounted cash-flow analysis, the number that combines the discount rate and the number of periods a cash flow is to be discounted. For example, given a 10% discount rate and five periods, the discount factor is $1/(1+0.10)^5 = 0.62$.

Discount Rate

The rate at which a future cash flow is discounted to determine its present value. The weighted average cost of capital is a common example.

Discounted Cash Flow (DCF)

The present value of a future cash flow, or flows. In the discounted cash-flow model of valuation, the sum of all future cash flows is an estimate of a company's present value. Discounting is necessary to account for the opportunity costs incurred through the passage of time—"a dollar today is worth more than a dollar tomorrow."

Distribution

An amount of money, similar to a dividend, that is paid to the partners of a master limited partnership according to their percentage ownership. For tax purposes, distributions usually have a large portion that is considered a return of capital rather than income.

Dividend

Cash distributed by companies to their shareholders. Dividends may occur quarterly, yearly, or on special occasions. Older, more established companies tend to pay out a large percentage of their profits, while newer, growth-oriented companies tend to pay low dividends or none at all. Dividends can also be distributed as stock, but this practice is not common.

Dividend Rate

The amount of dividends paid expressed as a percentage of earnings or more often as an absolute dollar amount.

Dividend Reinvestment Plan (DRIP)

An optional plan offered by some corporations that allows immediate reinvestment of dividends into additional shares, sometimes at a discount to the current market price. DRIPs can be an effective method of investing for those who don't need current income.

Dividend Yield

The dividends per share of a company over the trailing one-year period as a percentage of the current stock price. Dividend yield is often compared with the current yield of bonds, which is a bond's coupon divided by the bond's price.

Dollar Cost Averaging

A systematic, periodic investment of a fixed dollar amount. When investment prices fall, a greater amount of the investment (i.e., more shares) are purchased, and vice versa.

Dow Jones Industrial Average (DJIA)

An index of 30 large companies representing several industries. The DJIA (or "The Dow" for short) was first published in 1896 and is frequently used as a gauge of the overall stock market.

DuPont Equation

An equation that allows for in-depth analysis of a firm's return on assets (ROA) and return on equity (ROE). The DuPont equation provides information on a firm's profitability, asset utilization, and financial leverage. This increased breakdown of ROA and ROE inputs allows for a better understanding of a company's internal workings.

E

Earnings Per Share (EPS)

The amount of net income a company earned divided by the number of shares outstanding. For example, if a firm earned $1 million last year and had 100,000 shares of stock outstanding, its EPS would have been $10 for the year ($1 million/100,000 shares = $10).

Earnings Surprise

The difference between a company's actual financial results for a given period and what Wall Street analysts expected. Usually there is a share price increase for positive earnings surprises and a price decrease for negative earnings surprises, depending on the magnitude of the discrepancy.

Earnings Yield

The inverse of the P/E (price/earnings) ratio. For example, if the current price of a stock is $20, last year's earnings were $1 million, and there are 4 million shares outstanding, then the earnings per share is $0.25 ($1 million/4 million shares = $0.25), and the earnings yield is 1.25% ($0.25/$20 = 0.0125, 1.25%).

EBITDA

A financial metric representing earnings before interest, taxes, depreciation, and amortization. EBITDA can be a useful proxy for a company's gross cash flow.

Economic Moat

A framework used to measure a company's ability to maintain a competitive advantage for an extended period. (The term "economic moat" is derived from a phrase originally coined by Warren Buffett.) Think of a great company (and its profits) as a castle surrounded by a wide moat that attackers (competitors) would have an extremely difficult time crossing. Contrast this with a not-so-great, no-moat company whose competitors can attack with ease. The width of an economic moat (strength of competitive advantages) is crucial in determining how profitable a company is, and how long it can maintain this status. Common sources of economic moats include being the low-cost producer, benefiting from switching costs, having a network effect, and holding intangible assets such as patents, copyrights, and brands.

Economies of Scale

A desirable situation in which the cost per unit of production decreases as output increases. This occurs because of operating efficiencies usually caused by large fixed cost outlays for mass-production machinery, a large enough labor force to allow for specialization, or the ability to buy supplies in bulk for a lower price than competitors pay. Economies of scale can lead to a sizable economic moat that protects a company's profitability.

Enterprise Value

Calculated by adding a company's market capitalization to its debt minus cash. Enterprise value is a useful approximation for the "buyout value" of a company.

Equity Capital

The capital contributed by a company's shareholders. Its value can be found from the balance sheet by summing the additional paid-in capital and common stock accounts. Equity capital may also be used in reference to shareholders' equity, in which case it is calculated as assets minus liabilities. In other words, equity is the difference between the value of what a company owns and what it owes. In general, a company with greater equity capital than debt capital is considered more stable.

Excess Cash

1. *See Free Cash Flow.*

2. Cash held by a company not needed to operate its business.

Exchange-Traded Fund (ETF)

A stock-like security that is structured to mimic an index. ETFs are similar to index funds offered by mutual fund companies except that they trade on an exchange, which gives investors the ability to sell short, buy on margin, and engage in any other activity normally associated with a stock.

Ex-Dividend Date

The date on which you must be holding a stock to receive an upcoming dividend.

Exercise

The act of realizing the intrinsic value of an option that is in the money. When exercising a call option, this is accomplished by buying a stock at below market prices, and when exercising a put option, this is accomplished by selling a stock at above market prices.

Expenses

The costs of doing business such as labor, materials, and taxes.

Expiration

The date when an option contract becomes worthless. This occurs when the price of a stock did not rise above (as was expected by the holder of a call) or fall below (as was expected by the holder of a put) the strike price.

F

Fair Value Estimate

An estimate of a stock's intrinsic worth today. In a discounted cash-flow model, the fair value estimate is calculated by summing up the value of all future cash flows in terms of today's dollars.

Fat Pitch

An approach to investing that hinges on patience and quality over quantity. The name is derived from a baseball analogy—since there are no called strikes in investing, it can be advantageous to wait for a fat pitch (an excellent company selling at a reasonable price), then swing for the fences.

Fee-Based Planner

A financial planner who provides research and suggestions regarding the allocation of an investor's funds for a fixed fee (as opposed to trading commissions). It is important to be aware of a planner's incentives to ensure that you share the same goals.

Fidelity Magellan

The mutual fund managed by Peter Lynch from 1977 to 1990 that enjoyed well-above-average returns during his tenure.

Fiduciary Duty

The responsibility an executive has to act on behalf of a company and its shareholders in regard to financial matters.

Fisher, Philip

A successful investor and author best known for the book *Common Stocks and Uncommon Profits*. He achieved success through diligent research and a long-term mentality.

Five Forces Model

A framework developed by Harvard professor Michael Porter used to describe the external pressures a company faces. It consists of buyer and supplier bargaining power, the threat of new entrants and substitutes, and the intensity of rivalry among industry competitors.

Form 4

A statutory filing required by the SEC to disclose stock transactions by a shareholder owning 10% or more of a company's outstanding shares. These can be telling of significant stockholders' opinions about the stock they own.

Forward Price/Earnings (Forward P/E)

Next year's earnings divided by the current market price of a stock.

Framing Effect

A behavioral finance term used to describe how the use of a reference point can affect decisions.

Free Cash Flow

The cash a company generated from its core business operations minus the expenses incurred to keep the company running. Free cash flow is called "free" because it represents the amount of money that a company's management is free to pay out to shareholders or use to fund new opportunities without harming the existing business. It is calculated from the statement of cash flows by taking net cash provided by operating activities minus capital expenditures, which are listed in the cash flows from investing activities, also on the cash flow statement.

Free Cash Flow to Equity

One of two primary methods of discounted cash-flow analysis. This method measures free cash flows and discounts them by the cost of equity.

Full-Service Broker

A more expensive alternative to a discount broker that provides research and suggestions regarding the allocation of an investor's funds.

Fundamental Equity Risk Premium

The return above the risk-free rate required by investors for a given stock, usually calculated by taking into consideration "fundamental" risk factors such as cyclicality, the predictability of cash flow, and even management quality. The riskier the investment, the greater the required premium.

Funds from Operations (FFO)

The cash flow from a REIT's operations, similar to the earnings per share of a stock. FFO is calculated as earnings plus the noncash expenses of depreciation and amortization.

Future Value

The value of a cash flow today projected into the future, taking into account the effects of compounding.

G

General Partner

The company, public or private, that is responsible for the operations of a master limited partnership.

Graham, Benjamin

Author best known for *The Intelligent Investor*—a book regarded by many as the bible of value investing. Graham was also Warren Buffett's most influential mentor.

Gross Profit

Revenues minus the cost of goods sold (COGS). Gross profit is one of many measures of profitability.

H

Herding Behavior

A psychology term used to describe how investors will follow a stock tip or the advice of others under the assumption that others have more information than they do.

Hindsight Bias

The tendency to re-evaluate our past behavior surrounding an event or decision after knowing the actual outcome.

House Money

A behavioral finance term referring to the notion that certain money, depending on how it was made, is less or more valuable than other money. For example, people will commonly take more risk with house money that was won, as it is often considered less real or valuable than earned income.

I

In the Money

A term used to refer to a call option whose strike price is below the current market price, or a put option whose strike price is above the current market price. The larger these differences, the "deeper" in the money the option becomes, and the more profitable the position.

Income Statement

A financial statement showing the money a firm has brought in (its revenues), the amount of money it has spent (its expenses), and the difference between the two (its profit). The income statement, one of the three main financial statements, covers a company's performance over a specific time period such as three months or one year and answers the question, "How much did the company make?"

Individual Retirement Account (IRA)

A type of investment account that gives its owners certain tax benefits. IRAS come in two flavors— "traditional" and "Roth." The common trait between the two types is that income in the accounts is allowed to grow tax-free.

Inflation

The upward movement in the prices of goods over time. Currencies tend to lose their value, or purchasing power, over time. This is important to consider when making an investment. Although this number can vary tremendously, the target rate in the U.S. is about 3%.

Initial Public Offering (IPO)

The act of selling a portion of a company to the general public by making shares of stock available on a stock exchange. "Going public" often raises millions, or even billions, of dollars in new capital for the company to invest in its operations.

Insider Transaction

A stock transaction conducted by a person possessing important nonpublic information about a company, such as an upcoming merger, divestiture, or any other material event. These transactions are unfair to other investors and, therefore, illegal.

Intangible Asset

An asset without a physical presence, such as intellectual property, a government approval, a brand name, a unique company culture, or a geographic advantage. Because they are difficult to quantify, intangible assets are sometimes excluded from certain valuation techniques and ratios. *See Economic Moat.*

Interest

The price paid for borrowed funds, or received for loaned funds. In an investment, such as a bond, the investor is loaning money to a corporation and in return receives interest on the principal loaned. Simple interest is paid off as accrued, and compound interest accumulates on itself, resulting in interest on top of interest.

Interest Expense

The cost of borrowing recognized on a corporation's income statement. As companies borrow more, interest expense becomes more burdensome. In a downturn, this fixed cost can cause bankruptcy in extreme cases. A good measure of a company's ability to pay its interest expense is the interest coverage ratio, which is operating profits divided by interest expense. The greater this multiple, the better.

Interest Income

Income from securities held by a company often in the form of corporate debt and money market accounts.

Interest Shield

The use of debt capital, the interest on which is typically tax-deductible, in order to "shield" earnings from taxes.

Intrinsic Value

1. The underlying value of a company not necessarily reflected on any financial statement. It can be thought of as the value of the firm today plus all of its potential value expected to result from future growth.

2. The potential gain realized by exercising an option. It is the difference between the strike price of the option and the current market price of the underlying stock.

Intrinsic Value Approach

A long-term investing philosophy that focuses on the value added by a company over an extended period. An investor following this approach must be capable of patiently waiting out short-term fluctuations with the belief that eventually a company's underlying value will be realized.

Inventory

An asset on the balance sheet that represents the finished, in-process, or raw goods a company intends to sell. Normally, inventory is considered a liquid asset that is regularly converted into cash.

Invested Capital

Funds allocated to a particular investment. For example, shareholders invest capital (cash) in stocks expecting a good return on this capital. Within a company, capital is invested in machinery, buildings, and any other asset needed to grow the business. Return on invested capital is a very important metric when considering a company.

L

Leverage

1. The percentage of a company's costs that are fixed, calculated as fixed costs divided by fixed plus variable costs, and referred to as operating leverage. High operating leverage increases risk by making the company less flexible in economic downturns. However, when the business is doing well, high operating leverage allows profits to increase very quickly once fixed costs are met.

2. The amount of debt versus equity used to finance a company's operations. High debt versus equity increases profit potential, but the fixed payments associated with large amounts of borrowed capital can be a significant burden when a business is struggling.

Liability

A debt, such as a loan or principal on bonds, owed by a company usually to banks or to investors. Total liabilities, a line item on the balance sheet, can be a revealing metric in determining the financial health of a company. Liabilities can be calculated as a company's assets minus its equity.

Limit Order

A type of order placed with a broker for a stock transaction. The transaction is executed only if a stock trades below the named maximum buy price, or above the named minimum sell price.

Limited Partner

The public unitholders of a master limited partnership. Limited partners have limited control of the company, but their personal liability is also limited to their investment.

Long-Term Equity Anticipation Securities (LEAPS)

An option contract that has a long duration until expiration. This can be a safer method of predicting stock movement than traditional, shorter duration options because the additional time allows for greater price movement and less of a reliance on proper short-term timing. However, this added benefit is accompanied by a price tag that is often quite high.

Loss Aversion

A behavioral finance term used to describe the tendency to avoid selling declining stocks because of the unwillingness to accept defeat and admit a mistake.

Low-Cost Producer

A company that can deliver its goods or services at a lower cost than competitors can. Common ways to achieve this position are economies of scale and technology. This is one way for a company to form an economic moat.

Lynch, Peter

Managed the Fidelity Magellan Fund to well-above-average returns from 1977 to 1990 in addition to writing several revered investment books. Most of his success came from investing in companies early in their growth phase and staying within his circle of competence. He was a proponent of being aware of changes in your surroundings for signs of investment opportunities.

M

Margin

1. Total sales minus certain expenses, divided by total sales, expressed as a percentage. For example, the gross margin is the percentage of revenues that results in profit after costs of goods sold (COGS) have been subtracted.

2. A type of investment account in which the owner borrows against the value of the account.

Margin Call

Contact from a broker that a margin investment account has inadequate funds available. Investors using margin must maintain a certain portion of the account's value (often 50%) as equity with the other half being debt. If the equity's value falls below the required margin, which can occur when an account's value drops, then a margin call is made. Investors then have to put up more funds to boost the equity, or the broker will subsequently sell the investments held as collateral.

Margin of Safety

The discount an investor requires to a stock's fair value estimate before purchase to account for the uncertainties involved in valuing an investment. Smart investors require a margin of safety to account for the fact that their predictions may be wrong.

Market Capitalization

A company's total market price, calculated by multiplying the number of shares outstanding by the current price per share. This figure is often used when referring to the size of a company.

Market Order

A method of buying stock at the current market price. Generally, a market order gives a broker the go-ahead to purchase a security as soon as possible at the prevailing price.

Market Value

The most recent price quoted for a stock on an exchange.

Master Limited Partnership (MLP)

A publicly traded limited partnership. Similar to REITs, MLPs are exempt from corporate income taxes and pay out most of their cash flow in the form of distributions.

Maturity

The end of an investment period, most often applied to the date principal is returned in a bond investment.

Mental Accounting

The act of putting money into specific "buckets" for specific purposes.

Miller, Bill

Successful value investor with Legg Mason Funds who has consistently outperformed the market by buying stocks that typically do not fit the "value" mold.

Moat

See Economic Moat.

Modern Portfolio Theory

A statistical approach to portfolio management developed in the 1950s that tries to match a given risk tolerance (or aversion) with an optimal reward.

Monopoly

A situation where one company controls substantially all of a particular market. This can be achieved through the possession of a superior product, a patent, regulation, or, in unfortunate cases, by unsavory or even illegal business practices.

Mr. Market

A personification of the market created by Benjamin Graham. Mr. Market's often irrational and extreme mood swings allow the rational, patient investor opportune times to buy and sell investments.

Munger, Charlie

Chairman of Wesco Financial and partner of Warren Buffett at Wesco's parent company, Berkshire Hathaway. Munger is known for his terse satirical humor and, save for Buffett, is arguably the most intelligent investor of all time.

Mutual Fund

A financial instrument consisting of a basket of securities, usually stocks and bonds. A mutual fund typically includes a particular type of stock such as growth, large cap, small cap, value, and international to name a few. The main advantage of a mutual fund is investment diversification without excessive time and effort.

N

Narrow Moat

A rating used by Morningstar to describe a company that has a competitive advantage, but one that is relatively weak. Likewise, it can be used to describe a strong advantage that is not expected to last.

Nasdaq Composite Index

A stock index made of more than 3,000 companies traded on the technology-company-heavy Nasdaq stock exchange. "Nasdaq" is short for National Association of Securities Dealers Automated Quotations system.

Net Asset Value (NAV)

The value of a company derived by taking the total market value (not the book value) of its assets minus total liabilities.

Net Income

A company's total profit for a given time period, calculated as total revenues minus total expenses. This number may also be called "net profits," "the bottom line," or "net earnings."

Net Margin

Net income divided by total sales. Net margin (also known as net profit margin) is the percentage of every dollar in sales that translates to net income after all expenses have been subtracted. The higher this number, the more profitable the company.

Network Effect

A favorable competitive situation in which a company attracts additional customers by virtue of its existing customers. For example, as online auction firm eBay attracts more sellers, more buyers arrive, who in turn attract more sellers. It is an extremely desirable cycle, and one source of an economic moat.

New York Stock Exchange (NYSE)

One of the oldest and largest stock exchanges in the world. On an average day, more than 1 billion shares will be bought or sold on the exchange, which traces its origin back to 1792.

Nominating Committee

A part of a company typically responsible for nominating potential board members for election by shareholders.

Non-Interest-Bearing Liabilities

A liability that bears no interest rate. Non-interest-bearing liabilities typically appear due to accrual accounting. Examples include deferred revenue and accounts payable.

NOPAT

Net operating profit after tax. NOPAT is used to view a company's profitability as if it were not burdened by the cost of debt. This is what is typically used in the cash flow to the firm method of discounted cash-flow analysis.

Nygren, Bill

Successful value investor at Oakmark and Oakmark Select mutual funds, which have consistently outperformed the market.

O

Oligopoly
A situation in which a few firms dominate a certain market.

Operating Cash Flow
How much cash a company generates from its operations. Operating cash flow, which can be found in the top third of the statement of cash flows, can vary significantly from net income due to accrual accounting.

Operating Leverage
See the first definition of Leverage.

Operating Profit
Revenues minus the costs necessary to run the core businesses, such as cost of goods sold (COGS); selling, general, and administrative (SG&A) costs; depreciation and amortization; and research and development expenses. Operating profit is sometimes called EBIT (earnings before interest and taxes). It is a good indicator of the strength or weakness in the continuing operations of a company.

Oracle of Omaha
A common nickname for Warren Buffett.

Ordinary Income
An individual's income, such as wages and interest, that is taxed at ordinary income rates, as opposed to capital gains and dividends, which are taxed at their own rates.

Out of the Money
A term used to reference options whose strike price is below the current market price for puts and above the current market price for calls. Out-of-the-money options do not have intrinsic value.

Overconfidence
A behavioral finance term used to describe our tendency to think we are smarter, more talented, or more capable than we actually are.

P

Payout Ratio
The percentage of earnings that is paid to shareholders in the form of dividends.

PEG Ratio
An extension of the price/earnings ratio that accounts for earnings growth, calculated by dividing the forward P/E ratio by expected annual earnings per share (EPS) growth.

Pension Plan
A type of retirement plan set up by corporations that guarantees benefits for employees. In this scenario, the corporation bears the market risk,

whereas in a 401(k) retirement plan, benefits are based on employee contributions, and employees bear the market risk. 401(k) plans are quickly becoming the standard as pension plans are inherently inflexible and enormous costs can result.

Perpetuity Value
In a discounted cash-flow stock valuation, the value of a company beyond an explicit forecast period and into infinity.

Present Value
Today's value of future cash flows after being discounted by an appropriate discount rate. In a discounted cash-flow model, expected cash flows are discounted and then summed to find a company's current value. The opposite of this is future value—the present value is compounded (instead of discounted) for a certain number of periods at a particular rate to find an investment's worth in the future.

Present Value of Perpetuity
The value of a future perpetuity, discounted back to today's value. Calculating the present value of perpetuity is one of the final steps in performing a discounted cash-flow analysis.

Price/Book Ratio (P/B)
The market price of a company's outstanding stock divided by the company's book value. Book value is the total assets of a company less total liabilities, preferred stock, and intangible assets.

Price/Cash Flow
A stock's current price divided by the trailing 12-month operating cash flow per share. This is an indicator of a company's financial health.

Price/Earnings Ratio (P/E)
A stock's price divided by the stock's earnings per share. This is the most commonly referred to stock valuation metric.

Price/Sales Ratio (P/S)
A company's market capitalization divided by sales. The price/sales ratio represents the amount an investor is willing to pay for each dollar generated by a company's operations. This measure can be useful when the company in question has negative earnings or cash flow.

Principal
The par value of a bond that is paid to the lender (purchaser of the bond) upon maturity. In the case of a loan, such as a home mortgage, principal is the original amount loaned that is gradually amortized by the portion of each payment that is not interest.

Profit
Money generated in excess of money spent. This is why firms are in business. Gross profit and operating profit are common examples of profit measurements.

Prospectus

A legal document filed with the SEC (usually associated with an IPO) that outlines the purpose of the company, major risk factors, and planned use of the capital raised by the offering.

Proxy

An authorization through which a shareholder designates someone else (usually company management) to cast his or her vote in important company matters. The number of votes allowed per share of stock or whether any such votes exist will vary by company.

Proxy Fight

A dispute over a company matter that is taken to shareholders to decide. Proxy fights commonly occur in potential company takeover situations.

Proxy Statement

A statutory form required by the SEC that discloses various types of company information such as executive compensation, board of director nominations, and other issues that may or may not require a shareholder vote. Proxy statements are useful in gauging the long-term intentions of management. For example, will incentives given to management create intrinsic value for shareholders?

Public Filings

The various reports and documents required by law to be made available to investors. Common examples are 10-Qs and 10-Ks, which are collected and reviewed by the Securities and Exchange Commission (SEC).

Publicly Traded

A company is publicly traded when a portion of its shares is available for sale and purchase on a stock exchange. A firm becomes publicly traded through an IPO with the usual purpose of raising capital for a company.

Put

An option represented by a contract that allows the purchaser to sell a stock to a second party within a certain amount of time. The other party, or "writer of the put," is obligated to buy the stock, and is compensated for this risk by a premium—the price of the contract. The put holder will exercise the option only when the strike price of the put is more than the current market price. The difference between these two numbers less the premium paid is the put holder's gain.

Q

Qualified Dividend

Dividends from most domestic corporations and some foreign corporations that are eligible for the 15% dividend tax rate. Requirements include a minimum holding period and that the position was unhedged.

Quarterly Report
See 10-Q.

R

Rate of Return
The return of an investment divided by the original amount invested, usually stated in an annualized amount.

Ratio-Based Approach
The use of common financial ratios, such as P/E and P/B, to value stocks.

Real Estate Investment Trust (REIT)
Pooled investor funds used for investment in many types of real estate. REITs trade on an exchange like stocks, which makes them more liquid than direct real estate investment. Due to their favorable tax treatment, they are required to pay dividends regardless of share appreciation.

Real Return
The rate of return adjusted for inflation, calculated as the nominal (actual) rate minus the inflation rate. For example, if inflation last year was 3% and a return of 10% was realized on an investment, the real rate of return was only 7%.

Regret
In the context of behavioral finance, the disappointment or distress that influences our ability to distinguish a bad decision from a bad outcome.

Representativeness
A mental shortcut that causes us to give too much weight to recent evidence—such as short-term performance numbers—and too little weight to the evidence from the more distant past.

Required Rate of Return
The return required by investors to compensate for the risk they assume when purchasing debt or stock.

Restructuring Charges
Expenses that a company realizes as the result of a structural change caused by a shift in strategy, a merger or acquisition, or asset devaluation. Investors should be leery of companies that repeatedly use these supposedly "one-time" charges to hide larger operating issues.

Return on Assets (ROA)
A measure of a company's efficiency and profitability. Boiled down, it is calculated as net income divided by total assets. There is no rule as to what is a good ROA, so it is best to analyze this measure within the context of a firm's particular industry. ROA is usually stated as a percentage.

Return on Capital (ROC)
See Return on Invested Capital.

Return on Equity (ROE)
An efficiency measure calculated as net income from the income statement divided by shareholders' equity on the

balance sheet. ROE can also be calculated as ROA times a company's financial leverage. The purpose of this measure is to see how much profit the company is producing with money invested by shareholders. ROE is usually stated as a percentage.

Return on Invested Capital (ROIC)

Arguably the most important profitability measure, calculated as NOPAT divided by total assets, minus excess cash and non-interest-bearing liabilities. This is a good indication of how effectively a company allocates and uses its capital. ROIC is usually stated as a percentage.

Return on Stock

See Total Shareholder Return.

Revenue

A line item from the income statement that represents the dollar amount of goods and services sold by a company. Note that this does not necessarily represent the cash a company received because some sales are made on credit, which would increase the receivables account.

Revenue Recognition

The process by which revenue is earned and recorded by a company. Due to accrual accounting, when a company recognizes revenue can vary significantly from when a company collects the cash from selling its goods or services.

Risk-Free Rate

Typically refers to the rate of return on United States Treasury securities. Although theoretically possible, the U.S. government would have to go bankrupt for these bills, notes, and bonds to default. So far, this has never occurred.

Risk Premium

The additional return required by investors for taking on additional risk. The risk premium can be related to a variety of investments: the premium required on stocks versus bonds, the premium required for a particular stock over the general market (as in CAPM), or the premium of an investment over the risk-free rate.

Roth IRA

A type of individual retirement account (IRA) that allows for tax-free accumulation of savings. Investors who qualify can contribute aftertax dollars to Roth IRAs, and withdrawals are tax-free, subject to certain rules.

Royalty Trust

An investment vehicle that derives its income from royalties, typically on the production of natural resources. Royalty trusts can have very high yields, but those yields can vary significantly over time.

Ruane, Bill

A value investor taught by Benjamin Graham in the same classroom as Warren Buffett. Ruane is founder and chairman of Sequoia Fund, which has consistently beaten the S&P 500 Index.

Rule of 72

A shorthand method of estimating the number of years it will take for an investment to double in value at a given interest rate. It is calculated as 72/(interest rate). For example, an investment receiving 10% interest per year would approximately double in 7.2 years (72/10).

S

S&P 500 Index

A stock index composed of 500 large U.S. companies chosen based on market size, liquidity, and group representation. Like the Dow, the S&P 500 is often used to gauge the health of the overall stock market and as a benchmark for the performance of investment portfolios.

Securities and Exchange Commission (SEC)

The federal regulatory agency with the responsibility of protecting investors by ensuring fair transactions and adequate disclosure of relevant information in the financial markets.

Selective Memory

Remembering an event or action in a way that may be more favorable, and less accurate or objective, particularly if the event or action was painful. Selective memory can be a detrimental behavior when investing.

Self-Handicapping

Explaining any possible poor performance with a reason that may or may not be true.

Selling, General, and Administrative Expenses (SG&A)

Expenses found on the income statement that result from various corporate activities not directly associated with a product's cost, such as utility bills, payroll, advertising, leases for corporate headquarters, and others.

Share Buybacks

The purchase of a company's shares by the company itself. Buybacks are generally considered a shareholder-friendly action taken by management when it feels the price of company stock is below its intrinsic value. Buybacks lower the outstanding share count, increasing earnings per share, and thereby increasing the value of shares held by shareholders.

Shareholders

The owners of the stock of a company. Management should always strive to benefit shareholders by increasing the intrinsic value of their firms through the profitable allocation of resources. Shareholders have the responsibility to voice their opinion of management's actions by voting their proxies.

Shareholders' Equity

The estimated accounting value of a company. It is generally calculated as assets minus liabilities. In other words, equity is the difference between the value of what a company owns and what it owes.

Shares

The denomination of ownership in a company. The more shares you own of a company, the greater your ownership stake. Shares, or stocks, used to be represented by paper certificates, but these have been largely replaced with electronic accounts.

Shorting

A speculative venture that results in a gain when the price of a stock falls instead of rises. The stock is borrowed and immediately sold at current market prices. If the stock price drops as expected, the stock is repurchased at the new lower price and returned to the lender. Think of it as trying to sell high and buy low, in that order. Shorting is a risky way to make money since potential losses are unlimited, while gains are capped at the original sale price.

Special Dividend

A one-time dividend that is substantially larger than a normal dividend, usually reflecting an exceptionally strong earnings period, a desired change in the company's financial structure, or a company's inability to find adequate returns on a growing hoard of cash.

Microsoft's $32 billion ($3 per share) special dividend in 2004 is a good example of the latter.

Spin-off

An independent company created from a portion of an existing company that is sold as a whole unit, or through a public offering of shares. A company may cleave a portion of itself in order to focus on other parts of the business, or to capitalize on the high prices being paid in the stock market for the portion of the business being sold.

Statement of Cash Flows

A financial statement showing how much cash has gone in and out of a company over a specific time period, such as three months or one year. The statement of cash flows, which is one of the three main financial statements, adjusts for certain transactions that may affect income but do not result in cash flows.

Stewardship

A measure of how well company executives are doing their jobs, and whose best interests they have in mind. Increasing shareholder value should always be the supreme concern.

Stock

See Shares.

Stock Dividend

The distribution of additional shares to current shareholders instead of cash dividends. This method of paying shareholders is uncommon today.

Stock Split

A process whereby a company issues new shares to existing stockholders. The most common stock split is 2-for-1, which means that an investor who owned one share before the stock split will own two shares afterward, each at half of the old value. A stock split does not change the overall value of a company; it just changes the number of shares.

Stop-Loss Order

An order placed with a broker that designates a particular sell price for a stock that is below the current market price. Stop-loss orders are designed to limit an investor's loss.

Street Lag

A term coined by Peter Lynch referencing all the buying activity that has likely preceded a buy recommendation by a broker. Unfortunately, many brokers will not recommend a particular stock to their clients until there has been sufficient institutional purchasing, which validates the stock's "investment worthiness" in the broker's mind. By this time, the stock is often overpriced, which is precisely when you shouldn't buy.

Strike Price

The price at which an option allows the purchaser to either sell or buy the underlying security, usually a stock. The holder of a call option profits when the stock price rises above the strike price, whereas the holder of a put option profits when the stock price falls below the strike price.

Sunk Cost Fallacy

A behavioral finance theory stating that we are unable to ignore the "sunk costs" of a decision, even when those costs are unlikely to be recovered.

Supplier Power

One of Michael Porter's Five Forces that references the ability of suppliers to demand profitable prices for their goods and services. Any firm that is at the mercy of its suppliers will have a hard time making ends meet.

Sustainable Growth

The growth in earnings a company could theoretically achieve assuming current profitability and the dividend payout rate are held constant, calculated as ROE x (1 – payout ratio). *See Payout Ratio and Return on Equity.*

Switching Costs

Inconveniences or expenses a customer incurs in order to switch from one product to another. Companies want their customers to have high switching costs because this widens companies' economic moats.

Systematic Risk

Market risk that is not diversifiable. Systematic risk affects the valuation of all stocks through macroeconomic variables such as recessions and changes in monetary policy (interest rates) and fiscal policy (tax structure).

T

Taxable Account

An investment account not sheltered from taxes. This means you have to pay taxes on any interest payments or dividends, as well as on any capital gains you realize when investments are sold. With tax-deferred accounts, such as IRAs and 401(k)s, you can postpone the payment of these taxes.

Tax-Deferred

An account, such as an IRA or 401(k), that lets you postpone paying taxes on your earnings. Because more of your money works for you through compounding, tax deferral allows you to earn more over time.

Tax Rate

The percentage of earnings paid in taxes, calculated by dividing earnings before taxes by taxes paid.

Threat of Substitutes

One of Michael Porter's Five Forces that references the possibility of competitors creating a product that can effectively replace another firm's products. Optimally a company tries to create a product or service that is not easily replaced by a rival's offering.

Time Value

The value of an option that is based on the length of time until expiration. Time is important when valuing an option. The option holder wants to have more time between now and the option's expiration date to allow for the possibility of price changes. Time combined with a volatile stock makes the chance of an option becoming in the money much more likely. As an option reaches its expiration date, the premium investors are willing to pay diminishes until it reaches zero on expiration day.

Total Return

The return of a stock based on its price appreciation as well as its dividends. A common measure of total return is called the holding period return and is calculated as current price minus purchase price (capital gains), plus dividends.

Transparency

The degree to which a company's financial and operational disclosures are clearly presented. Legal jargon and diversion tactics can severely limit the transparency of a company's financial statements. Generally, the more opaque the language in disclosures, the more the company has to hide. On the other hand, the Berkshire Hathaway annual report is a great example of transparent disclosure.

U

Unitholder

An investor who holds units in a master limited partnership. Unitholders are essentially the same as shareholders in a corporation. They receive distributions (similar to dividends) and can benefit from price appreciation of their units.

Unsystematic Risk

The unique risk inherent to a specific company or stock that can be offset through diversification (also known as diversifiable risk).

V

Valuation

The process of determining how much a company is worth. There are many ways to value a company. The method focused on in these workbooks is the discounted cash-flow (DCF) method.

Volatility

The degree of fluctuation in the price of a stock. High volatility indicates that the stock's price has experienced significant ups and downs in the past, whereas low volatility indicates that the stock's price has been relatively stable. A common measure of volatility is beta, which measures price change relative to a market index. A beta greater than one indicates that the stock is more volatile than the index, whereas a beta less than one indicates that the stock is less volatile than the index.

W

Wanger, Ralph

The successful investor who in 1992 founded Columbia Wanger Asset Management, which invests using value-oriented principles.

Weighted Average Cost of Capital (WACC)

The weighted average of the cost of debt and the cost of equity for a given company. When performing a cash flow to the firm method of discounted cash-flow analysis, all future cash flows are discounted by this percentage and then summed to determine present value. Higher WACCs indicate a greater uncertainty surrounding future cash flows, which appropriately results in lower valuations of those future cash flows.

Whisper Stock

A stock that is getting a lot of subtle attention as a potential breakout performer. Tips received through a whisper, or any other method for that matter, should be taken with skepticism and carefully analyzed on a fundamental basis before considering investment.

Whitman, Marty
The chairman of Third Avenue Funds who has achieved great success through value investing.

Woodstock for Capitalists
Common name for the Berkshire Hathaway annual shareholder meeting, as well as the name of a documentary profiling this event. It attracts thousands of attendees every year, and is chaired by Warren Buffett and Charlie Munger.

Writer
The seller of an option contract. The writer has the obligation to provide the underlying stock, in the case of a call, and to buy the underlying stock, in the case of a put, from the buyer of the written contract. Writing options is risky because of the large loss potential with the upside limited to the premium—the price of the contract.

Y

Yield
See Dividend Yield.

Formulas Reference

Valuation Ratios

Market Capitalization = Stock Price × Shares Outstanding

Enterprise Value = Market Capitalization + Debt − Cash

P/E = Stock Price ÷ EPS = Market Capitalization ÷ Total Company Profits

Earnings Yield = 1 ÷ P/E = EPS ÷ Stock Price

PEG = Forward P/E ÷ 5-Year EPS Growth Rate

P/S = Stock Price ÷ Sales Per Share = Market Capitalization ÷ Total Sales

P/B = Stock Price ÷ Book Value Per Share =
Market Capitalization ÷ Total Shareholder Equity

Book Value Per Share = Total Shareholder Equity ÷ Shares Outstanding

P/CF = Stock Price ÷ Operating Cash Flow Per Share =
Market Capitalization ÷ Total Operating Cash Flow

Accounting

Assets = Liabilities + Equity

Gross Profit = Net Revenue − Cost of Sales

Operating Income = Gross profit − SG&A − Depreciation − Amortization −
Other Operating Expenses − Restructuring Expenses

Net Income = Operating Income − Tax Expense − Interest Expense −
Any Other Nonoperating Expense

continued…

continued...

Basic EPS = Net income ÷ No. of Basic Wtd. Avg. Shares Outstanding

Diluted EPS = Net Income / No. of Diluted Wtd. Avg. Shares Outstanding

Free Cash Flow = Operating Cash Flow − Capital Expenditures

Company Efficiency and Financial Health Metrics

Inventory Turnover = Cost of Sales ÷ Average Inventory

Accounts Receivable Turnover = Revenue ÷ Average Accounts Receivable

Accounts Payable Turnover = Cost of Sales ÷ Average Accounts Payable

Total Asset Turnover = Revenue ÷ Average Total Assets

Current Ratio = Current Assets ÷ Current Liabilities

Quick Ratio = (Cash + Accounts Receivable + Short-Term or Marketable Investments) ÷ Current Liabilities

Cash Ratio = (Cash + Short-Term or Marketable Investments) ÷ Current Liabilities

Debt/Equity = (Short-Term Debt + Long-Term Debt) ÷ Total Equity

Interest Coverage = Operating Income ÷ Interest Expense

Gross Margin = Gross Profit (or Loss) ÷ Sales

Operating Margin = Operating Income (or Loss) ÷ Sales

Net Margin = Net Income (or Loss) ÷ Sales

Free Cash Flow Margin = Free Cash Flow ÷ Sales

ROA "traditional" = (Net Income + Aftertax Interest Expense) ÷ Average Total Assets

Aftertax Interest Expense = $(1 - \text{Tax Rate}) \times$ Interest Expense

ROA "DuPont" = Asset Turnover × Net Profit Margin

ROE "traditional" = Net Income ÷ Average Shareholders' Equity

ROE "DuPont" = Asset Turnover × Net Profit Margin × Asset/Equity Ratio

ROIC = Net Operating Profit, After Taxes (NOPAT) ÷ Invested Capital (IC)

Net Operating Profit, After Taxes (NOPAT) = Operating Profit $\times (1 - \text{Tax Rate})$

Invested Capital (IC) = Total Assets − Excess Cash − Non-Interest-Bearing Current Liabilities

Cash Return = (Free Cash Flow + Net Interest Expense) ÷ Enterprise Value

Time Value of Money and DCF

Approximate Time Required for Money to Double = 72 ÷ Annual Rate of Return

Future Value = Present Value $\times (1 + i)^N$

i = Interest (your rate of return or interest rate earned)
N = Number of Years (the length of time you invest)

Present Value of CF in Year N = CF at Year N $\div (1 + R)^N$

CF = Cash Flow
R = Required Return (Discount Rate)
N = Number of Years in the Future

continued...

continued...

Perpetuity Value = $CF_n \times (1 + g) \div (R - g)$

CF_n = Cash Flow in the Last Individual Year Estimated
g = Long-Term Growth Rate
R = Discount Rate, or Cost of Capital

Weighted Average Cost of Capital (WACC) = (Weight of Debt)(Cost of Debt) + (Weight of Equity)(Cost of Equity)

Graham's Intrinsic Value Formulas

Value = Current (Normal) Earnings $\times$
(8.5 + Twice the Expected Annual Growth Rate)

Approximate P/E = (8.5 + Twice the Expected Annual Growth Rate)

Expected Growth = (Stock Price − 8.5) $\div$ (2 $\times$ Current Earnings)

Dividends and Sustainable Growth

Dividend Yield = Annual Dividends Per Share $\div$ Current Stock Price

Payout Ratio = Dividends Per Share $\div$ EPS

Required Retention Ratio (R3) = Expected Growth Rate $\div$ ROE

Sustainable Growth = ROE $\times$ (1 − Payout Ratio)

Cost of Growth = R3 $\times$ Normalized EPS

Excess Earnings Yield = (Normalized EPS − Dividends Per Share − Cost of Growth) $\div$ Current Share Price

Total Expected Return = Dividend Yield + Expected Profit Growth + Excess Earnings Yield

More Stock Workbooks in the Morningstar Investing Series

How to Select Winning Stocks
Learn how to interpret financial statements, place a value on business, and find financially strong companies for potential investment.

How to Refine Your Stock Strategy
Go beyond good stock-picking to become a great stock investor. Learn the techniques of great investors, our fat-pitch strategy, and more.

Also Learn the Ins and Outs of Successful Fund Investing with Morningstar Mutual Funds Workbooks

the Right Mutual Funds
eginners searching for funds
ill best meet their investing
ives.

Diversify Your Fund Portfolio
For investors with a little experience who want to improve their skills, techniques, and portfolios.

Maximize Your Fund Returns
For experienced fund investors looking for new ways to improve the value of their portfolios.

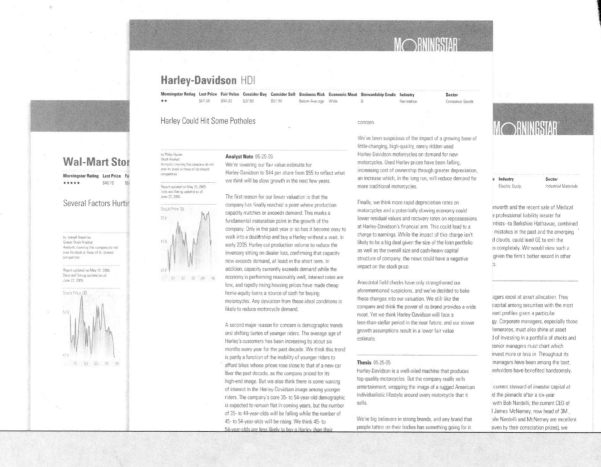